First World War
and Army of Occupation
War Diary
France, Belgium and Germany

40 DIVISION
Divisional Troops
Royal Army Medical Corps
136 Field Ambulance
1 June 1916 - 29 May 1919

WO95/2602/2

The Naval & Military Press Ltd
www.nmarchive.com
Published in association with The National Archives

Published by

The Naval & Military Press Ltd

Unit 10 Ridgewood Industrial Park,

Uckfield, East Sussex,

TN22 5QE England

Tel: +44 (0) 1825 749494

www.naval-military-press.com

www.nmarchive.com

This diary has been reprinted in facsimile from the original. Any imperfections are inevitably reproduced and the quality may fall short of modern type and cartographic standards.

© **Crown Copyright**
Images reproduced by permission of The National Archives, London, England, 2015.

Contents

Document type	Place/Title	Date From	Date To
Heading	WO95/2602/2		
Heading	40th Division 136th Field Ambulance Jun 1916-1919 May		
Heading	No. 136 F.A. June 1916.		
Miscellaneous	From:- O.C. 136 Field Ambulance	03/07/1916	03/07/1916
War Diary	Bullswater Camp Nr. Pirbright	01/06/1916	21/06/1916
War Diary		16/06/1916	30/06/1916
Heading	Medical Services War Diary of O.C. 136th Field Ambulance. For month of July 1916. (Volume II)		
War Diary	Bruay	01/07/1916	04/07/1916
War Diary	La Beuvriere	05/07/1916	31/07/1916
Heading	40th Div. 136th Field Ambulance. August 1916.		
War Diary	La Beuvriere	01/08/1916	31/08/1916
Heading	40th Div. 136th Field Ambulance. Sept 1916.		
War Diary	La Beuvriere map France sheet 36B 1/40,000 D.16.a.5.3.	01/09/1916	05/09/1916
War Diary	La Beuvriere	06/09/1916	30/09/1916
Heading	40th Div. 136th Field Ambulance. Oct. 1916.		
War Diary	La Beuvriere	01/10/1916	12/10/1916
War Diary	Braquemont L.25.b.2.5	12/10/1916	29/10/1916
War Diary	Braquemont	30/10/1916	31/10/1916
War Diary	Bruay J.16.c.2.0	31/10/1916	31/10/1916
Heading	40th Div 136th Field Ambulance. Nov 1916.		
War Diary	Bruay J.16.c.2.0.	01/11/1916	01/11/1916
War Diary	Boirin T.9.b.5.9.	01/11/1916	02/11/1916
War Diary	Neuville	02/11/1916	04/11/1916
War Diary	Boffles	04/11/1916	04/11/1916
War Diary	Frohen-Le-Petit	05/11/1916	15/11/1916
War Diary	Boffles	15/11/1916	16/11/1916
War Diary	Occoches	17/11/1916	17/11/1916
War Diary	Bouquemaison	17/11/1916	18/11/1916
War Diary	Haute Visee	19/11/1916	22/11/1916
War Diary	Beauval	22/11/1916	23/11/1916
War Diary	Houdencourt	23/11/1916	24/11/1916
War Diary	Vauchelles Les. Quesnoy	24/11/1916	30/11/1916
Heading	40th Div. 136th Field Ambulance. Dec 1916.		
War Diary	Vauchelles-Le-Quesnoy	01/12/1916	10/12/1916
War Diary	Camp 12 K.33.b	10/12/1916	25/12/1916
War Diary	Camp 17.	26/12/1916	31/12/1916
Heading	40th Div. 136th Field Ambulance Jan 1917.		
War Diary	Camp 17 G.8.b.	01/01/1917	01/01/1917
War Diary	Camp 17.	02/01/1917	17/01/1917
War Diary	Camp 17 G.8.b	17/01/1917	28/01/1917
War Diary	Sailly-Laurette	29/01/1917	29/01/1917
War Diary	J.36.d.8.3.	30/01/1917	31/01/1917
Miscellaneous	Report on Work done in Rancourt sector by 136 F.A. 25-12-16 to 27-1-17.	25/01/1916	25/01/1916
Map			
Heading	40th Div. 136th Field Ambulance. Feb 1917.		
War Diary	Sailly Laurette	01/02/1917	01/02/1917

War Diary	J.36.d.3.3.	01/02/1917	10/02/1917
War Diary	Camp 21 G.3.a.9.8.	10/02/1917	28/02/1917
Heading	40th Div. 136th F.A. Mar 1917.		
War Diary	Camp 21 G.3.a.9.8	01/03/1917	08/03/1917
War Diary	Suzanne G.8.d.9.2.	09/03/1917	20/03/1917
War Diary	Hem H.8.a	21/03/1917	22/03/1917
War Diary	Hem	23/03/1917	31/03/1917
Heading	40th Div. 136th F.A. April 1917.		
War Diary	Hem. H.8.a	01/04/1917	07/04/1917
War Diary	Manancourt V.13	07/04/1917	07/04/1917
War Diary	Manancourt	08/04/1917	20/04/1917
War Diary	Manancourt V.13	20/04/1917	21/04/1917
War Diary	Manancourt	22/04/1917	23/04/1917
War Diary	Fins	23/04/1917	30/04/1917
War Diary	Manancourt U.13.B.8.2	10/04/1917	27/04/1917
Heading	40th Div. 136th F.A. May 1917.		
War Diary	Fins	01/05/1917	31/05/1917
Miscellaneous	Evacuation Scheme of Front Line 40th Division. Headquarters, 136, Field Ambulance. R.A.M.C. App I.	10/05/1917	10/05/1917
Operation(al) Order(s)	40th Division R.A.M.C. Operation Order No. 26. Appendix II.	11/05/1917	11/05/1917
Miscellaneous	Evacuation Scheme of Left and Centre Brigades, Front Line. 40th Division. Appendix III.	14/05/1917	14/05/1917
Map			
Heading	No. 136th F.A. June 1917.		
War Diary	Fins V.12.B	01/06/1917	20/06/1917
War Diary	Fins	21/06/1917	30/06/1917
Miscellaneous	Evacuation Scheme of Front Line, 40th Division. Appendix No. 1.	01/06/1917	01/06/1917
Miscellaneous	Evacuation Scheme of Front Line, 40th Division. Appendix No. 2.	12/06/1917	12/06/1917
Miscellaneous	To:-A.D.M.S., 40th Division. Appendix No. 3	12/06/1917	12/06/1917
Miscellaneous	Evacuation Scheme of Front Line, 40th Division. Appendix 4.	17/06/1917	17/06/1917
Map			
Heading	No. 136. F.A. July 1917.		
War Diary	Fins	01/07/1917	29/07/1917
Heading	No. 136 F.A. Aug. 1917.		
War Diary	Fins V.18.d	01/08/1917	21/08/1917
War Diary	Moislain C.18.a	22/08/1917	31/08/1917
Heading	No. 136. F.A. Sept. 1917		
War Diary	Moislains C 18	01/09/1917	30/09/1917
Heading	Medical Services War Diaries of A.D.M.S. 40th Division. O.C. 135th Field Ambulance. O.C. 136th Field Ambulance. O.C. 137th Field Ambulance. For month of October, 1917 Vols XVII.		
Heading	136 Fd Amb. Vol 17. Oct. 1917.		
War Diary	Moislains C.12.d.0.5.	01/10/1917	31/10/1917
Heading	No. 136 F.A. Nov. 1917.		
War Diary	Lucheux T.16	01/11/1917	16/11/1917
War Diary	Gouy-En-Artois P.18.d.2.5	17/11/1917	17/11/1917
War Diary	Gomiecourt A.23.d.0.4	17/11/1917	19/11/1917
War Diary	Barastre O.15.b.8.6	20/11/1917	22/11/1917
War Diary	Trescault	24/11/1917	26/11/1917
War Diary	Lechegges	26/11/1917	30/11/1917

Miscellaneous	136 Field Ambulance 40 Divn. Volume 18. Appendix II.		
Miscellaneous	40th Division. R.A.M.C. Corps. Appendix III.	28/11/1917	28/11/1917
Miscellaneous	40th Division. R.A.M.C. Corps. Appendix III.	29/11/1917	29/11/1917
Heading	No. 136 F.A. Dec 1917.		
War Diary	Bienvillers Au-Bois	02/12/1917	02/12/1917
War Diary	Hamegincourt	03/12/1917	31/12/1917
Heading	No. 136 F.A Jan 1918.		
War Diary	Hamegincourt S.29.d.9.6	02/01/1918	31/01/1918
Heading	No. 136 F.A. Feb 1918.		
War Diary	Hamelincourt S.29.d.9.6 (51.B)	05/02/1918	12/02/1918
War Diary	Blaireville (X.4.d.8.2) 51 C.	15/02/1918	24/02/1918
Heading	136th Field Ambulance Mar 1918.		
War Diary	Blaireville 51c X.4.c.9.8.	01/03/1918	23/03/1918
War Diary	Ayette 57D F11 b 9.1	23/03/1918	24/03/1918
War Diary	Bucquoy 57D L.11.a.8.8.	24/03/1918	24/03/1918
War Diary	Minchy-Au-Bois 57D E.6.a.9.6.	24/03/1918	26/03/1918
War Diary	Pommier 51c N.25.c.6.8.	26/03/1918	26/03/1918
War Diary	Habarcq 51c K.8.c.2.8.	27/03/1918	27/03/1918
War Diary	Sombrin 51C D.23.b.4.4.	27/03/1918	29/03/1918
War Diary	Bajus Lens 1/10000 I F 8.1	29/03/1918	30/03/1918
Heading	136th Field Ambulance. April 1918.		
War Diary	Bajus (Lens 1F)	01/04/1918	01/04/1918
War Diary	Sailly-En La Lys. S.17.a.7.3. Sheet 36.	02/04/1918	09/04/1918
War Diary	Doulieu	09/04/1918	09/04/1918
War Diary	Vieux Berquin	10/04/1918	10/04/1918
War Diary	Hazebrouck	10/04/1918	10/04/1918
War Diary	4th St Razeele	11/04/1918	11/04/1918
War Diary	Borre	12/04/1918	12/04/1918
War Diary	Hondeghem.	13/04/1918	13/04/1918
War Diary	Staple	14/04/1918	14/04/1918
War Diary	Tilques	16/04/1918	21/04/1918
War Diary	Boisdinghem	22/04/1918	30/04/1918
Heading	No. 136 F.A. May 1918.		
Miscellaneous	16th Divn. No. A. 533.	07/06/1918	07/06/1918
War Diary	St. Momelin	01/05/1918	01/05/1918
War Diary	Waemers Cappel	02/05/1918	29/05/1918
War Diary	Enquin 6 E (Calais 13)	30/05/1918	30/05/1918
Heading	136th F.A. June 1918.		
War Diary	Enquin Sur Baillon Calais 13 6D	01/06/1918	24/06/1918
War Diary	Lart Hazebrouck	25/06/1918	25/06/1918
War Diary	5A-4A Ebblinghem Sheet 27 T.18.c.8.7.	28/06/1918	29/06/1918
Heading	136th F.A. July 1918.		
War Diary	Ebblinghem T.18.d.2.7	01/07/1918	31/07/1918
Heading	136th F.A. Aug 1918.		
War Diary	Ebblinghem 27/T.18.c.8.7	01/08/1918	31/08/1918
War Diary	Wallon Cappell 36A/C.5.a.5.9	31/08/1918	31/08/1918
Heading	136th F. Amb. Sept. 1918.		
War Diary	Wallon Cappell 36 A/C.5.a.5.9	01/09/1918	08/09/1918
War Diary	36 A/F.29.d.6.9	10/09/1918	18/09/1918
War Diary	La Brielle Farm 36 A/L.5.a.5.8	19/09/1918	19/09/1918
War Diary	Proven 27/E.6.d	19/09/1918	19/09/1918
War Diary	Welsh Farm 28/B.14.c.5.5	21/09/1918	30/09/1918
Heading	136th F.A. Oct. 1918.		
War Diary	Welsh Farm. 28/B.14.c Central	01/10/1918	07/10/1918
War Diary	Steenwerck 36/A.37.d.5.5	10/10/1918	17/10/1918

Type	Location	Start	End
War Diary	Steenwerck	18/10/1918	18/10/1918
War Diary	Armentieres 36/B.20.c.5.8	19/10/1918	24/10/1918
War Diary	Wambrechies 36/E.21.d.1.2	25/10/1918	27/10/1918
War Diary	37/B.19.b.4.4	28/10/1918	31/10/1918
Heading	136th F.A. Nov. 1918.		
War Diary	37/G.19.b.3.2	01/11/1918	09/11/1918
War Diary	Pecq 37/H6 Central	10/11/1918	13/11/1918
War Diary	Pecq. 37/H.6.a Cent.	13/11/1918	14/11/1918
War Diary	Pt. Lannoy 37/G.19.b.3.2	15/11/1918	23/11/1918
War Diary	Mouvaux 36/F.14.d.2.4	24/11/1918	30/11/1918
Heading	No. 136 F.A. Dec 1918.		
War Diary	Mouvaux T.14.d.1.3	01/12/1918	31/12/1918
Heading	40 Div Box 2418 No 136 F.A. Jan 1919.		
War Diary	Mouvaux 36/T.14.d.1.3	01/01/1919	31/01/1919
Heading	No 136 Field Ambulance Feb 1919.		
War Diary	Mouvaux 36/T.14.d.1.3	01/02/1919	28/02/1919
Heading	136th F.A. Mar. 1919.		
War Diary	Mouvaux	01/03/1919	31/03/1919
Heading	136th F.A. April 1919.		
War Diary	Croix	01/04/1919	25/04/1919
Heading	No 136 Field Ambulance. May 1919.		
War Diary	Croix (Nord)	06/05/1919	29/05/1919

WO95/26022

40TH DIVISION

136TH FIELD AMBULANCE
JUN 1916 - ~~DEC 1918~~
1917 MAY

No. 136 F.A.

June 1916.

From:- O.C 136° Field Ambulance
To:- A.G Office at the Base.

3rd July 16

Army Form C.2118. of
136° Field Ambulance, herewith.

J E Rowan Robinson
Lt Col, RAMC
O.C 136th Field Amb

136th Field Ambulance Army Form C. 2118
R.A.M.C. VOL 1

WAR DIARY
INTELLIGENCE SUMMARY
(Erase heading not required.)

Mob. France 36 B
40,000

Place	Date	Hour	Summary of Events and Information	Remarks and references to Appendices
Bullswater Camp N. Pirbright	1-6-16		Under instructions of G.O.C. one Officer left for Havre as billeting officer, the rest of the Ambulance entraining at L.S.W. Rly station FARNBOROUGH at 5.40 a.m.	then
	2-6-16		The Unit left BULLSWATER COMMON CAMP - ALDERSHOT district for FARNBOROUGH STN at 12.30 a.m. The Ambulance, having on a previous occasion had the opportunity of practicing, entrained without any difficulty in one train. SOUTHAMPTON was reached at 7.30 a.m. The Unit disentrained and personnel consisting of the A.S.C. and 30 R.A.M.C. including N.C.Os and 3 (Three) Officers was embarked on the HUNSLET by 12 mid-day. The HUNSLET sailed at 5 p.m. The remainder of the Unit embarked on the ST. TUDNO and left SOUTHAMPTON at 6 p.m., arriving at HAVRE at 2 a.m. June 3rd.	
	3-6-16		The unit marched to Shed "R" and assisted in unloading the HUNSLET. On completion of disembarkation the unit proceeded to Camp No. 3 HAVRE	then
	4-6-16		At 24 hours June 4th unit entrained at Gare de Marchandise	the

1875. Wt. W593/826 1,000,000 4/15 J.B.C. & A. A.D.S.S./Forms/C. 2118.

WAR DIARY / INTELLIGENCE SUMMARY

136th Field Ambulance Army Form C. 2118
R.A.M.C.

Mat 36 B
France 1/40,000

Place	Date	Hour	Summary of Events and Information	Remarks and references to Appendices
	4.6.16		to LILLERS. The horses were watered during 1/2 hours stop at ABBEVILLE and hot water was obtained for tea.	H.P.R.
	5.6.16		LILLERS was reached 16 o'clock June 5th and the Unit proceeded to the village of HURIONVILLE, which had been apportioned to it for billeting purposes.	H.P.R.
	5.6.16 to 10.6.16		June 5 – June 6th was entirely occupied in improving sanitary arrangements in the village.	H.P.R.
	10.6.16 to 21.6.16		Following instructions from the A.D.M.S., "A" Section proceeded to the front for instructional purposes. One half section to BETHUNE attached to 45th F.A. One half section to LA BOURSE attached to 46th F.A. with the exception of one cook who was retained at the main dressing station, all the Officers, N.C.Os & men did a turn of duty in the trenches and at the advanced dressing station.	H.P.R.
	21.6.16		The course of instruction was completed on June 21st when "A" Section, reunited at BETHUNE, proceeded to BRUAY. "B" Section relieved "A"	H.P.R.
	16.6.16		On instruction from A.D.M.S. 10th Division, on June 16th one Officer and 15 N.C.Os & men proceeded to AUCHEL to take over the hospital from the 37th F.A.	H.P.R.
	17.6.16		Further instructions from A.D.M.S. June 17th a party of 7 N.C.Os and men with the entire transport and equipment of "C" Section, together	H.P.R.

136 Field Ambulance Army Form C. 2118
Rgme.

WAR DIARY
or
INTELLIGENCE SUMMARY
(Erase heading not required.)

Place	Date	Hour	Summary of Events and Information	Remarks and references to Appendices
Map. France 36 B 1/40,000	17.6.16		with 2 motor ambulances also proceeded to AUCHEL.	ꝗRꝚ
	19.6.16		A second Officer proceeded to AUCHEL on June 19th and the remainder of the unit proceeded from HURIONVILLE to BRUAY, arriving at 12.30am. by instruction of the ADMS	ꝗRꝚ
	24.6.16		O.C. "C" Section AUCHEL reports satisfactorily of work carried out at 1st Corps Hospital.	ꝗRꝚ
	26.6.16		Following instructions from A.D.M.S. 40th Division, A & C Sections are to hold their bearer sub-divisions in readiness to move off at short notice for duty where required. A complete bearer division will be formed by one section of 135 F. Amb. in conjunction with "A" & "C" Sections.	ꝗRꝚ
	26.6.16 to 30.6.16		The rest of the month was occupied in converting one of the huts into a Dressing Station, and the treatment and evacuation of the sick and wounded of 120th Infantry Brigade.	ꝗRꝚ

J W Broadbottom
Lt Colonel
O.C. 136 Fld Amb

Confidential

Medical Services

War Diary

of

O.C. 136th Field Ambulance.

For Month of July, 1916.

(Volume II)

COMMITTEE FOR
MEDICAL HISTORY OF THE WAR
Date 5 - SEP. 1916

Secret

Vol. II.

WAR DIARY
or
INTELLIGENCE SUMMARY
(Erase heading not required.)

Army Form C. 2118

136 Field Ambulance

M.G.A. France 36 B / 40,000

Place	Date 1916	Hour	Summary of Events and Information	Remarks and references to Appendices
BRUAY	July 1st		B. Section returned from the course of instruction with 4.5 - 4.6 Field Ambulances. The tent subdivision of B. Section proceeded to AUCHEL to take over the I" Corp Hospital from C. Section. Tent Subdivision joined Headquarters of the Ambulance at BRUAY.	Orders and Returns 1st Ren
	July 2		C. Section handed over I" Corp Hospital to B. Section and proceeded to join 4.5 - 4.6 Field Ambulances for the course of instruction. Church Parade Service.	J.H.O.
	July 3		D.C. 136 F. Amb. under instruction from A.D.M.S. 10th Div. proceeded to LA BEUVRIERE D. 17 a 4.5 to commune latrini for A Section I" Corps Rest Station	J.H.O.
	July 4		A Section and tent subdivision of B. Section proceeded from BRUAY to LA BEUVRIERE to duty at A Section I" Corps Rest Station. Tent Subdivision of B Section handed over I" Corps Hospital at AUCHEL to Officer i/c Scottish Hospital AUCHEL and proceeded to LA BEUVRIERE.	J.H.O.

WAR DIARY or INTELLIGENCE SUMMARY

Army Form C. 2118

Vol. II

136 Field Ambulance
May France 36b 40,000

Place	Date 1916	Hour	Summary of Events and Information	Remarks and references to Appendices
LA BEUVRIERE	July 5th		Day was occupied in taking over 1st Corps Rest Station	Appx
	July 6		Lt. Col. Pullan of 136 Field Ambulance was admitted to hospital. A.D.M.S. thanks in accommodation for 300 N.C.O's + men + 16 Officers at the station	
			1st Corps Rest Station. Remaining Officers 13 Other Ranks 188	Appx
				Appx
	July 7		Remaining Officers 14. O.R. 196	Appx
	8		Remaining Officers 14. O.R. 195. Lt. Goss F.A. 40th Divisional Sanitary	Appx
	9		A.D.M.S. 40th Division inspected 1st Corps Rest Station	Appx
			Remaining Officers 14. O.R. 203	
	10		Remaining Officers 13. O.R. 200	Appx
	11		C. Section returned to Headquarters of Field Ambulance having completed two weeks of instruction with 1 So. Mid. Field Ambulance. Remaining Officers 13. O.R. 181	Appx

Sept
Vol. II.

WAR DIARY
or
INTELLIGENCE SUMMARY

(Erase heading not required.) MAP France 36 c 1/40,000

Army Form C. 2118

136 Field Ambulance

Place	Date 1916	Hour	Summary of Events and Information	Remarks and references to Appendices
LA BEUVRIERE	July 12th		Remains officer 13 O.R. 176	Y&R
"	13th		Remains officer 12 O.R. 176. to MC 16 for grenade School at LA BEUVRIERE.	Y&R
"	14th		Remains officer 11, O.R. 170.	Y&R
"	15th		Under instruction from S.D.M.S 1st Corps I inspected the Campani Ground & inspected this morning by the 5th Brigade R.F.A. and reported on its Sanitary condition. Remains officer 12 O.R. 199 from A.D.M.S 10th Division C Section proceeded to under instruction to be attached to 137 Field Ambulance.	Y&R
"	16th		BRAQUEMONT R.19 The Transport of C Section returned the same day as there was no accommodation for it at BRAQUEMONT Remains officer 12 O.R./82	Y&R
"	17th		Paid the patients in hospital Remains officer 11 O.R. 193	Y&R

Army Form C. 2118.

136 Field Ambulance

Vol. II

WAR DIARY
or
INTELLIGENCE SUMMARY

(Erase heading not required.) Map ref 36 b 1/40,000

Instructions regarding War Diaries and Intelligence Summaries are contained in F.S. Regs., Part II. and the Staff Manual respectively. Title Pages will be prepared in manuscript.

Place	Date 1916	Hour	Summary of Events and Information	Remarks and references to Appendices
LA BEUVRIÈRE	Jan 18		Remaining Officers 12 O.R. 188	F.O.R.
	19th		Remaining Officers 15 O.R. 222	F.O.R.
	20th		Remaining Officers 14 O.R. 251	F.O.R.
	21st		Remaining Officers 13 O.R. 243	F.O.R.
	22nd		Remaining Officers 16 O.R. 245 — Under instruction from A.D.M.S. 40th Division this Motor Ambulance was put to BRACQUEMONT to be attached to 137 Field Ambulance.	
	23		The G.O.C 40th Division accompanied by A.D.M.S 40th Division inspected A Section 1 Corps Rest Station. Remaining Officers 15 O.R. 243	F.O.R.
	24		Remaining Officers 15 O.R. 270 CAPT P.S. GAFFIKIN	F.O.R.
	25		Remaining Officers 14 O.R. 252. Capt Gaffikin having reported was deemed to be taken on the strength from 25 instant.	F.O.R.
	26		Remaining Officers 12 O.R. 287	F.O.R.

WAR DIARY or **INTELLIGENCE SUMMARY**

Army Form C. 2118

136 Field Ambulance

Vol II

Place	Date 1916	Hour	Summary of Events and Information	Remarks and references to Appendices
LA BEUVRIÈRE	July 27		Remaining Officers 13. O.R. 288. The following instruction received from A.D.M.S. 40th Divn. "Please note that Lt. R.N. CRAIG R.A.M.C. will assume permanent duty as Officer in Medical charge of 19th Field Amb: from 28th inst."	✓ FCR
	28		Remaining Officers 11. O.R. 287. Lt. P. BLACK R.A.M.C. proceeded to CALONNE to relieve Lt. SPENCE R.A.M.C. On O.C. 13 Batt. Surrey Regt.	✓ FCR
	29.		Remaining Officers 11. O.R. 278. D.D.M.S. 1 Corps inspected Officers Rest Station.	✓ FCR
	30		Remaining Officers 9+2=/2 O.R. +232. The following reinforcement demand was sent in to-day. Wanted to complete: One Senior Officer. One Corporal. three privates.	✓ FCR
	31.		Remaining Officers 9. O.R. 200. G.O.C. 32 Division visited the Rest Station.	✓ FCR

40th Div.

136th Welsh Ambulance.

August 1916

COMMITTEE FOR THE
MEDICAL HISTORY OF THE WAR
Date -9 OCT. 1916

WAR DIARY or INTELLIGENCE SUMMARY

Army Form C. 2118

136 Field Ambulance
France 36.- 1/40,000

Volume VIII

Place	Date 1916	Hour	Summary of Events and Information	Remarks and references to Appendices
LA BEUVRIERE	August 1st		Remaining Officers 11 O.R. 209	Forwarded at Report 1st & Return
	2		Remaining Officers 11 O.R. 225	Form
	3		Remaining Officers 11 O.R. 221	Form
	4		Remaining Officers 13 O.R. 248	Form
	5		Remain Officers 14 O.R. 253	Form
	6		The cinematograph performance was given in the theatre to-day for the patients in the Rest Station, a first one for the troops at LABEUVRIERE. Two performances were given from to-day one was free for the children of the village, for the other a small charge was made to cover the expenses.	Form
	7		Remaining Officers 12 O.R. 251	Form
	8		Remaining Officers 14 O.R. 265	Form
			Remaining Officers 13 O.R. 266	Form
	9		Remaining Officers 14 O.R. 263	Form

WAR DIARY
or
INTELLIGENCE SUMMARY

Army Form C. 2118

Volume III   Secret   136 Field Ambulance
from 36° 1:40,000

Place	Date 1916	Hour	Summary of Events and Information	Remarks and references to Appendices
LA BEUVRIERE	August 10th		O.C. Section of this Unit reformed Headquarters at 5 p.m. today. Remained Open 16 O.R. 280	4/22
	11th		D.D.M.S. I Corps visited the Rest Station this afternoon. Remained Open 14 OR 276	4/22
	12th		I Corps Commander inspected the Rest Station. He did not think that the accommodation was sufficient. It was suggested that the Mill near the Chateau should be used by the Patients as a Recreation Room. Remained Open 11 O.R. 285	4/22
	13th		A.D.M.S. 40th Div visited the Rest Station. Remained Open 14 O.R. 277	4/22
	14		Remained Open 12 O.R. 243	4/22
	15		Under instructions from A.D.M.S. 40th Division Lt. MORRIS left Headquarters to take over temporary charge of 83 Sanitary Section. Remained Open 14 O.R. 269	4/22

WAR DIARY

Secret

136 Field Ambulance

Volume III

Army Form C. 2118

INTELLIGENCE SUMMARY France 36.b / 40.000

Place	Date 1916.	Hour	Summary of Events and Information	Remarks and references to Appendices
LABEUVRIERE	Aug. 16th		Remaining officers 14 O.R. 951	MRPR
	17th		Lt. CRELLIN took over the duties of Medical Officer in charge of 40th Divisional Ammunition Column. He is acting as M.O. of the troops of 136 Field Ambulance billeted here. A.D.M.S. 10th Division examined the patients in the Rest Station belonging to the 40th Division and marked a number of them as temporarily unfit for service in the trenches. The CTE 1 Corps visited the Rest Station. Remaining officers 12 O.R. 270	MRPR
	18th		Remaining officers 12 O.R. 258. D.D.M.S. I Corps inspected the Rest Station with a view to erecting a new hut C.E. I Corps being on the ground. Points of kitchen accommodation. The site selected is on the west side of the kitchen. Many new huts are being built in line with the Canteen on the west side of it. These are to be taken over as the Recreation Room of the Rest Station. The Huts has now been taken over as the Recreation Room of the hospital. The work is to be made for all the patients in the hospital. The work is to be carried out by the patients themselves under R.E. supervision. Pictures for the material to be acquired have been submitted.	MRGR

1875 Wt. W593/826 1,000,000 4/15 J.B.C. & A. A.D.S.S./Forms/C. 2118.

Army Form C. 2118

WAR DIARY
or
INTELLIGENCE SUMMARY
(Erase heading not required.)

Volume III

136 Field Ambulance
France 38½ / 20,000

Instructions regarding War Diaries and Intelligence Summaries are contained in F. S. Regs., Part II. and the Staff Manual respectively. Title Pages will be prepared in manuscript.

Place	Date 1916	Hour	Summary of Events and Information	Remarks and references to Appendices
LA BEUVRIERE	August 19		Remaining officers 11 O.R. 229	Appx
	20		Remaining officers 16 O.R. 247	Appx
	21		Remaining officers 16 O.R. 255	
			There has been luncheon with the idea of reducing the bare sum of the expenses than has been purchased with the money for the luncheon was obtained from the Rest Station. It is proposed to see the bill for this from they have been made by the Canteen fallen in and the proceeds to be returned to the Canteen.	Appx
	22		Remaining officers 15 O.R. 252	
	23		The I Corps Concert "the Very lights" gave a performance in the Unit when in town thoroughly the patients enjoyed it thoroughly a great success.	Appx
	24		Remaining officers 14 O.R. 246 the Very lights gave their second performance this evening. It was again much appreciated by the patients.	Appx
	25		Remaining officers 12 O.R. 243	Appx
			Remaining officers 12 O.R. 243	
	26		Remaining officers 11 O.R. 254	Appx
			A short performance was given by the Very lights at which the Army Corps commander attended	

Army Form C. 2118

136 Field Ambulance
France 36 1/40,000

WAR DIARY
or
INTELLIGENCE SUMMARY
(Erase heading not required.)

Volume VII

Place	Date 1916	Hour	Summary of Events and Information	Remarks and references to Appendices
LA BEUVRIÈRE 27	Aug		Remaining Officers 7 O.R. 267	Appx
	28		Remaining Officers 7 O.R. 977. Under instruction from A.D.M.S. 40th Division Lt. P. BLACK RAMC took over medical charge of 181st Brigade R.F.A. from Lt. WYPER RAMC. Lt. A.H. MUIR RAMC reported his arrival for duty with this unit at 5.30 pm today.	Appx
	29		Remaining Officers 10 O.R. 247. Under instruction from A.D.M.S. 40th Division 200 men from Bearer Section of this unit proceeded to LES BREBIS to work with an R.E. lookout party.	Appx
	30		Lt. MORRIS rejoined headquarters of this unit at 11am today. Remaining Officers 9 O.R. 264	Appx
	31		Remaining Officers 8 O.R. 10. Under instruction from D.D.M.S. I Corps I am proceeding to AIRE today to make arrangements for the accommodation of the officers in the I Corps Rest Station. The Buildings I understand have been selected by the D.D.M.S. I Corps	Appx

1875 Wt. W593/826 1,000,000 4/15 J.B.C. & A. A.D.S.S./Forms/C. 2118.

140/1/54

40" 12s

136th Field Ambulance

COMMITTEE FOR THE
MEDICAL HISTORY OF THE WAR
Date 30 OCT. 1916

Secret

Army Form C. 2118

Volume IV

136 Field Ambulance
40th Division
France 36 J
1 to 500

WAR DIARY
or
INTELLIGENCE SUMMARY
(Erase heading not required.)

Instructions regarding War Diaries and Intelligence Summaries are contained in F. S. Regs., Part II. and the Staff Manual respectively. Title Pages will be prepared in manuscript.

Place	Date 1916	Hour	Summary of Events and Information	Remarks and references to Appendices
LA BEUVRIERE map France Sheet 36A Sheet 36B 1:40,000 D.16.a.5.3	June 1st		Remaining Officer 9 O.R. 281. Proceeded to AIRE again to-day to continue making preparations to take over the building as an Officers Rest Station. The main building is to accommodate from patients the annexes patients are to be billeted in houses adjoining.	Lt Col Brown Officer i/c Lt Col Brown
	2d		Remaining Officer 9 O.R. 286.	HrcR
	3d		Remaining Officer 11 O.R. 263. A.D.M.S 40th Division inspected the patients of the 40th Division at the Rest Camp Shots, at which the band of 608 by A.S.C.M.T. played, were held to-day also a concert was given in the evening for the benefit of the patients. 136 F.Amb. v. 608 by A.S.C. M.T. there was also a football match 136 F.Amb won by two goals to nil.	HrcR
	4th		Remaining Officer 10 O.R. 257. The move of the Officers Rest Station from the Chateau at LA BEUVRIERE to AIRE was completed to-day.	HrcR
	5th		Remaining Officer 10 O.R. 285. Inspected the new Officers Rest Station at AIRE.	HrcR

Secret

Army Form C. 2118

136 Field Ambulance
3 to 13 Dec 1916

WAR DIARY
or
INTELLIGENCE SUMMARY
(Erase heading not required.)

Volume IV

France 36 - 40.000

Place	Date	Hour	Summary of Events and Information	Remarks and references to Appendices
LA BEUVRIERE	1916 Sept 6		Running Officer 13 O.R 964. Pte MUIR R.A.M.C posted to 231 Field Company Officer LES S BREBIS to take over the duties of Lieut A.E. HOCKETT R.A.M.C. who has been granted leave from 7th to 21st Sept 16. Lt J.E. EVANS went for duty with 136 Field Ambulance at 5.30 hr to-day	HQRR
	8th		Running Officer 12 O.R 974.	HQRR
	8th		Joined the Rest Station at AIRE and inspected them to the west.	HQRR
	9th		Running Officer 12 O.R 964. A convoy was held in the Recreation Hall. Running Officer O.R	
	10th		A Small Dressing Station - Medical Inspection Room has been opened at LABEUVRIERE for the purpose of treatment the forward of the Grenade School and of any other units stationed at LABEUVRIERE who have no medical officer attached to this Dressing Station at present consists of two rooms & one hitherto at any time be retained.	HQRR
			W.O in found attending to the PO. Running Officer 8 O.R 978 A.D.M.S Tour and the Rest Station
	11th		Running Officer 9 O.R 984	HQRR
	12th		I Coy Commander accompanied by D.D.M.S inspected the Rest Station Running Officer 9 s. R 261	HQRR
	13th		Running Officer 9 s. R 274. Divided with 18 C.C.S. + 136 Fd Amb at SARLANDY. 136 Fd Amb to us.	HQRR

1875 Wt. W593/826 1,000,000 4/15 J.B.C. & A. A.D.S.S./Forms/C. 2118.

WAR DIARY or INTELLIGENCE SUMMARY

(Erase heading not required.)

Army Form C. 2118

Sent:
136 Field Ambulance
A.D.S. 2 Division
France 36.c 40.000

Volume IV

Instructions regarding War Diaries and Intelligence Summaries are contained in F.S. Regs., Part II. and the Staff Manual respectively. Title Pages will be prepared in manuscript.

Place	Date 1916	Hour	Summary of Events and Information	Remarks and references to Appendices
LA BEUVRIERE	Sept 14th		Remaining Officers 10 O.R 276	JRR
	15		Remaining Officers 10 O.R 278	
			The following instructions received from A.D.M.S 40th Division.	
			O.C. 136 F.Amb.	
			It is proposed that you will send next week Return 137 F. Ambulance on the L.D.O.S pretty early in October. Will you kindly arrange with O.C 137 F. Amb. for an interchange of 1 Officer 2 Sergts 1 Cpl and 19 Men on the 16th inst. for the purpose of instruction in their duties at LOOS Rects and both Rest Stations respectively.	
			D.H.Gun	
			14.9.16	
			(Sgd) A.G. Sutton	
			A D.M.S 40th Division	
	16		I proceeded to NOEUX LES MINES to day to cope with O.C. 137 F. Amb.	JRR
			Remaining Officers 9 O.R 261	
			Capt J.O.S BEVERIDGE, 1 Sergt 1 Corporal and nine from 137 F.Amb arrived to day. They are being instructed in their duties at the Rest Station at 5 pm.	JRR
	17th		Capt Houston 2 Sgts 1 Cpl & 19 men left head quarters at 1.30 pm to day to be attached to 137 Field Ambulance for instruction in the duties in the LOOS Sector.	JRR
			Officers Remaining 9 O.R 271	

# WAR DIARY or INTELLIGENCE SUMMARY

Army Form C. 2118

136 Field Ambulance
10th Division

Volume IV

Place	Date 1916	Hour	Summary of Events and Information	Remarks and references to Appendices
LA BEUVRIERE	Sept 18th		Remaining Officer 9 O.R. 287. Jorsett Officer Rest Station at AIRE today & remained there for the night. The Ballroom is to be hacked and two baths are being purchased. The latrine is to be boarded on instead of using canvas.	
	19th		Remaining Officer 9 O.R. 264. Lt. A.H. MUIR having been posted for duty with 3rd Division is struck off the strength of this unit from to-day.	
	20.		Remaining Officer 9 O.R. 286. The Officer i/c men of 137 Field Ambulance returned to their headquarters to-day and gave their first performance this evening.	
	21.		Remaining Officer 9 O.R. 264.	
	22		Remaining Officer 9 O.R. 268.	
	23.		Remaining Officer 7 O.R. 266.	
	24.		Remaining Officer 4 O.R. 258. Took in Month at Swet 18 CCS. 136 Field Amb won by H Gate in 2.	

WAR DIARY
or
INTELLIGENCE SUMMARY

(Erase heading not required.)

Army Form C. 2118

Volume IV
Secret

136 Field Amb
H.Q. 1st Division
France 36° 40000

Place	Date 1916	Hour	Summary of Events and Information	Remarks and references to Appendices
LA BEUVRIERE	Sept 25		Remaining Officers 4 O.R 271	YPER
	26"		Remaining Officers 6 O.R 251	YPER
	27		Remaining Officers 9 O.R 278	YPER
	28		Remaining Officers 10 O.R 276	YPER
	29		Usual weekly inspection of the Field Ambulance at 5.30pm	YPER
			Remaining Officers 11 O.R 286	
	30"		Remaining Officers 11 O.R 293	
			The personnel of the Ambulance is distributed as follows:	
			Officers Rest Station at AIRE — Officers 1 O.R 20	
			Attached to 137 F. Amb — 1 20	
			Attached to 231 by R.E — 1 22	
			Divisional Laundry — 1	
			B.D.S.R.E. I Carter (with 2nd F. Amb) — 1	
			Attached 135 F. Amb (bath) — 1	
			9 O.R to O.R.S at AIRE yesterday and returned this morning. Satisfactory progress is being made with the bath house	

J.Attwood Mathews
Lt Col Comm
O.C 136 F.Amb

140/1815

40th Divn.

136th Field Ambulance

Oct. 1916

COMMITTEE FOR THE
MEDICAL HISTORY OF THE WAR
Date -9 DEC. 1916

WAR DIARY or INTELLIGENCE SUMMARY

Army Form C. 2118

136 Field Ambulance
110th Division

Volume V

Place	Date 1916	Hour	Summary of Events and Information	Remarks and references to Appendices
LA BEUVRIERE	Oct 1st		R 17 a.1.5. Remaining Officers 9 O.R 288	
	Oct 2		Remaining Officers 9 O.R 288. 20 O.R left Headquarters of this unit at 8.30 am to-day Capt. McCARTER and 20 O.R left Headquarters of this unit at 8.30 am today to relieve its hasty down duty with 137 Field Ambulance. Capt HOUSTON and 20 O.R returned to Headquarters of this unit at 6.30 pm to-day. Remaining Officers 7 O.R 280	J/A Sgrant Brown 1st O.R Rayne
	Oct 3		Lt E EVANS left to-day at 8.30 am to join 3rd Division for duty. He is struck off the strength of this unit from to-day. Officers Remain 10 O.R 967	Mase
	Oct 4		Remaining Officers 10 O.R 246.	J.M.R.R
	Oct 5		Remaining Officers 11 O.R 283	J.M.R.R
	Oct 6		Remaining Officers 10 O.R 978	J.M.R.R
	Oct 7		Remaining Officers 10 O.R 280	J.M.R.R
	Oct 8		Remaining Officers 15 O.R 288	J.M.R.R

WAR DIARY
or
INTELLIGENCE SUMMARY

Army Form C. 2118

136 Field Ambulance
Lt Col Stevenson
France 40 000

Place	Date 1916	Hour	Summary of Events and Information	Remarks and references to Appendices
LA BEUVRIERE	6.4.16		Remaining Officers 14 O.R 288 Following instructions received from A.D.M.S. 10th Division. 137 Field Ambulance will be relieved on the LOOS, 14 BIS, HULLUCH Section by 136 Field Amb. and will take over the Johan Rest Station at AIRE. LA BEUVRIERE and Officers Rest Station. O.C.'s Field Ambulances concerned details of relief to be arranged between 6 p.m. 19th inst and reported to the officer. Relief to be completed by 6 p.m. 19th inst and 14 O.R to be attached to 136 Field Ambulance the following which will be found by 137 Field Ambulance (i) 1 Officer 1 S.M. 2 Cpl and 14 O.R to be attached to 136 Field Ambulance (ii) 1 Officer for Divisional Laundry BETHUNE. (iii) 1 S.M. and 20 O.R working party for 231 by R.E. or LES BREBIS (iv) 1 Driver and Horse car for D.D.M.S Office at LA BUISSIERE. Remaining Officers 11 O.R 266. Proceeded to head quarters 137 Field Ambulance to make arrangements regarding relief	ApCR

Secret—

Volume V

WAR DIARY
or
INTELLIGENCE SUMMARY

(Erase heading not required.)

Army Form C. 2118

Issue 20,000 136 Field Ambulance
20th Division

Instructions regarding War Diaries and Intelligence Summaries are contained in F. S. Regs., Part II. and the Staff Manual respectively. Title Pages will be prepared in manuscript.

Place	Date 1916	Hour	Summary of Events and Information	Remarks and references to Appendices
LA BEUVRIERE	June 11th		Officers remaining 11 O.R. 234. St MORRIS and 35 O.R. proceeded to Walqueton at 1.30 pm to say Capt EDWARDS and 20 OR from 137 Field Ambulance arrived at the headquarters of this Ambulance at 4.30 pm	HPR
	12th		The handing over of the Rest Station to 137 Field Ambulance was completed this morning. The remainder of the Unit proceeded to BRAQUEMONT and took over the duties from 137 Field Ambulance	
BRAQUEMONT L28.6.25			Officers and nursing stations Josied the advanced dressing station at PHILOSOPHE and St PATRICKS and the afmt and took over at 4.00S O.R. sick 53 O.R wounded 10 Officers sick the duties of A.D.M.S. temporarily Col. LUTHER being took over the team proceeded to leave	HPR
	13th		Remaining Officers sick on O.R. sick 60 wounded 13 Three advanced dressing stations are in charge of the Unit — vis at Philosophe L28.a.3.0 St PATRICK S.8.35.a.37. St GEORGES S.23.b.68	HPR

1875 Wt. W593/826 1,000,000 4/15 J.B.C. & A. A.D.S.S./Forms/C. 2118.

Secret
Column V

WAR DIARY of 136 Field Ambulance
INTELLIGENCE SUMMARY
Army Form C. 2118
40th Division

Appendix IV

Place	Date	Hour	Summary of Events and Information	Remarks and references to Appendices
BRAQUEMONT L.25.6.95.d1/3	1916 2.6.95		Between PHILOSOPHE and St GEORGES there are three dug outs which are collectively known as HALF WAYHOUSE G.21.a.10.0. Four orderlies are doing duty there, they assist in carrying the cases from St GEORGES to PHILOSOPHE. Quite close to HALFWAY HOUSE is a battle aidpost which has been constructed. When it is completed it will accommodate 18 lying down cases. Patients are evacuated from St GEORGES both day & night by motor by & trolley and by means of wheeled stretchers to PHILOSOPHE. At the A.D.S. St PATRICKS the normal procedure is to evacuate at night time only except in urgent cases when a car may be sent at any time. The distribution of the personnel is as follows — PHILOSOPHE 2 N.C.O's 18 O.R. St PATRICKS 1 N.C.O 16 O.R. St GEORGES 1 N.C.O 17 O.R. The number at St GEORGES includes orderlies who scrubby floors dug outs Relieve by, at CHALK PIT dug out, there is 1 N.C.O - 11 men. The duties of these men are to look after cases from Regimental aid posts to PHILOSOPHE. The remainder of the personnel is at the nursing station at BRAQUEMONT.	

WAR DIARY or INTELLIGENCE SUMMARY

Army Form C. 2118

Secret — 136 Field Ambulance
Volume V — H.Q 45th Division

Place	Date 1916	Hour	Summary of Events and Information	Remarks and references to Appendices
BRAQUEMONT L.25.c.2.5 Bar 14"				
	15		Remaining Officers wounded 2. O.R Sick 49 wounded 18	ffrrr
			Visit St GEORGES	
	16		Remaining Officers 2 wounded 2 sick. O.R Sick 56 wounded 27	ffrrr
	17		Remaining Officers wounded 3 sick 3. O.R Sick 40 wounded 19	ffrrr
			Remaining Officers wounded 3 sick 2. O.R Sick 59 wounded 45	ffrrr
	18		Visit PHILOSOPHE - ST GEORGES	
			Remaining Officers wounded 3 sick 5. O.R Sick 53 wounded 38	ffrrr
	19		Remaining Officers wounded 1 sick 4. O.R Sick 61 wounded 28.	ffrrr
	20.		Remaining Officers wounded 1 sick 4. O.R Sick 63 wounded 20	ffrrr
			Orders about Dressing Station at PHILOSOPHE - ST GEORGES	ffer
			Instruction of Sanitaria. Ventilation. Clothing	
	21	9am	Remaining Officers wounded 1 sick 6 O.R Sick 63 wounded 20.	
	22	9-	Remaining Officers wounded mi sick 4 O.R Sick 53 wounded 18	ffrrr
	23	9-	Remaining Officers wounded 1 Sick 3. O.R Sick 55 wounded 19	ffrrr
	24	9am	Remaining Officers sick 2. O.R Sick 50 wounded 88.	ffrr
	25	9-	Remaining Officers sick 3 O.R Sick 64 wounded 32.	ffrrr

Secret

WAR DIARY or **INTELLIGENCE SUMMARY**
(Erase heading not required.)

Army Form C. 2118

of 136 Field Ambulance 40th Division

Volume V

Place	Date 1916	Hour	Summary of Events and Information	Remarks and references to Appendices
BRAQUEMONT L.25-6	25.6.2.5 26.10.16	9 am	Remaining sick 8 Br 6 wounded 2 OR sick 57 wounded 15. H.P.R. Under instructions from A.D.M.S. 40th Division 136 Field Ambulance will be relieved by 73rd Field Ambulance on Oct 30th and March to their destination on Oct 31st. I accompanied an officer from 73rd Field Ambulance round the advanced dressing stations with the exception of St Patricks. H.P.R.	
	27.10.16	9 am	Remaining Officers sick 3 O.R. sick 48 wounded 12. A.D.S. St Patrick's was handed over to day to a detachment of 73rd Field Amb. (attached to 73 Fd Amb) 2 N.C.O.s and 13 men of 73 F.Amb arrived to day and were distributed for duty at PHILOSOPHE, St GEORGES and CHALK PIT, NUNNERY, HALF WAY HOUSE. The detachment of 137 Field Ambulance attached to 136 F.Amb for duty returned to 1. ABEUVRIERE to day. H.P.R.	
	28.10.16	9 am	Remaining Officers sick 4, O.R. sick 50 wounded 13. H.P.R.	
	29.10.16	9 am	Capt Houston returned off leave today. Remaining Officers sick 4, O.R. sick 45 wounded 19. 73rd Field Ambulance is relieving 136 F.Amb at A.D.S. PHILOSOPHE, A.D.S. St GEORGES, HALFWAY HOUSE (CHALK PIT) today. H.P.R.	

WAR DIARY or INTELLIGENCE SUMMARY

Army Form C. 2118

136 Field Ambulance
1.0 "Division
36 B

Secret
Volume V

(Erase heading not required.)

Place	Date 1916	Hour	Summary of Events and Information	Remarks and references to Appendices
BRAQUEMONT	30.10.16	12.30 pm	Officers remaining Sections 3 O.R. Sect 4, 8 wounded 9. The Dressing station at BRAQUEMONT was handed over to 73rd Field Ambulance to-day by Mulkay. All the patients were transferred to 73rd F. Amb. JBA	
	31.10.16	9 am	Officers O.R. Remaining Out.	
BRUAY J.16.c.2.0		10.30 9 am	The Unit paraded at 7.30 am and marched at 8 am for BRUAY the proceeding of a Field General Court Martial was brought back at 3pm to-day 69320 Pte KEMP was returned to the Ranks and fined £1 for Drunkenness	

J Morrow Authorgon
Lt Col Command
OC 136 F Amb

140/267

40th Div

136th Field Ambulance

COMMITTEE FOR THE
MEDICAL HISTORY OF THE WAR
Date −3 JAN. 1917

Nov. 1916

Army Form C. 2118

136th Aust 736 Field Ambulance
No. ? Devriem

36 B

WAR DIARY
or
INTELLIGENCE SUMMARY
(Erase heading not required.)

Volume VI
Army Form C. 2118, Part II. Title Pages

Instructions regarding War Diaries and Intelligence Summaries are contained in F.S. Regs., Part II. and the Staff Manual respectively. Title Pages will be prepared in manuscript.

Place	Date 1916	Hour	Summary of Events and Information	Remarks and references to Appendices
BRUAY S16c20	1.11.16	9 a.m.	Permanent Officers and O.R. Out. The Unit marched with the 119th Brigade. The Starting Point was J.15c07 at 9.13 a.m. Destination BOIRIN T96.5.9. — The place was reached at 2.30 p.m.	
BOIRIN T965a.		9.30	The N.C.O.'s and Men marched with No. 1 Field Amb.	
	2.11.16	9 a.m.	MAP Ref France/10E.0/80 LENS Remaining O.R. Side 3 The unit marched with 119 Brigade. Starting point 8a at MARQUAY village 10.23 a.m. Destination NEUVILLE	YPER
NEUVILLE		1.15 p.m.		YPER
"	3.11.16	9 a.m.	Remaining O.R. Side 6 Sick evacuated to St POL. Two hrs. taken away during the night. Parties were searching for them all day without success. YPER	
BOFFLES	4.11.16	9 a.m.	Remaining O.R. Side 10 The Unit marched with the Brigade to BOFFLES Sick evacuated to No. 6 Stationary Hospital FREVENT YPER	
FROHEN LE PETIT	5.11.16		Remaining O.R. Side 5 The unit marched with the Brigade to FROHEN-LE-PETIT when they were billeted on the South side of the River L'AUTHIE	

WAR DIARY or INTELLIGENCE SUMMARY

Army Form C. 2118

136 Field Ambulance
40th Division
France 100,000 LENS

Volume VI

Place	Date 1916	Hour	Summary of Events and Information	Remarks and references to Appendices
FROHEN-LE-PETIT	6.11.16	9—	Remaining O.R. 114	
			The unit is occupied in interring the standing battalion of the village and in billets.	
			his returnees from 119th Brigade. ABR	
"	7.11.16		Remaining O.R. 12	
			Evacuated an over keen pmt. to 2/19 C.C.S. at DOULLENS. ABR	
"	8.11.16		Remaining O.R. 15 L/C HEWITT proceeded to No.4 C.C.S. for ordinary duty ABR	
"	9.11.16	Pomided	Remaining O.R. 17 L/ASHBY proceeded to England on leave ABR	
"	10.11.16		Remaining O.R. 20 ABR	
"	11.11.16		Remaining O.R. 19 Capt. McCARTER returned from leave ABR	
"	12.11.16		Remaining O.R. 20 ABR	
"	13.11.16		Remaining O.R. 20 ABR	
"	14.11.16		Remaining O.R. 21	
"	15.11.16		Remaining O.R. 2	
			Received instructions from A.D.M.S. 114 Brigade that unit proceeded to BOFFLES	
			under instruction left at 3pm. ABR	
BOFFLES	16.11.16		Arrived BOFFLES at 11pm.	
			Remaining O.R. 14 PULLAN was sent to 2/19 C.C.S. Grey & Mullett Men in the second line two officers	
			& Qm. PULLAN were evacuated as Q. & D. Mullet ABR	
OCCOCHES	17.11.16		Men been evacuated as O.R. 7	
			Remaining O.R. 7 Unit proceeded to OCCOCHES	
BOUQUEMAISON	18.11.16		BOUQUEMAISON Remaining O.R. 2 ABR	

Army Form C. 2118

Secret
Volume VI

WAR DIARY
or
INTELLIGENCE SUMMARY

(Erase heading not required.)

Instructions regarding War Diaries and Intelligence Summaries are contained in F.S. Regs., Part II. and the Staff Manual respectively. Title Pages will be prepared in manuscript.

136 Field Ambulance
N O h Division
From LENS

Place	Date 1916	Hour	Summary of Events and Information	Remarks and references to Appendices
BOUQUE MAISON HAUTE VISEE	19.11.16	am	Unit marched from BOUQUEMAISON to HAUTE VISEE from Remains O.R 6	
"	20.11.16		Remains O.R 9 yrs	
"	21.11.16		Remains O.R 16 yrs	
BEAUVAL	22.11.16		Unit marched from HAUTE VISEE to BEAUVAL Remains O.R 4 man	
HOUDENCOURT	23.11.16		Unit marched to HOUDENCOURT Remains O.R 6 yrs	
VAUCHELLES LES QUESNOY	24.11.16		Unit marched to VAUCHELLES LES QUESNOY from Remains O.R 3. Capt MCARTER and 20 O.R rejoined unit from No 9 C.C.S MCA.	
"	25.11.16		Remains O.R 13 man	
"	26.11.16		Remains O.R 11 K L HEWITT rejoined unit from 24 C.C.S from	
"	27.11.16		Remains O.R 10 On route to here from 28.11.16 to 8.12.16 CAPT GASKIN in the meantime taken charge of the unit from	

1875 Wt. W593/826 1,000,000 4/15 J.B.C. & A. A.D.S.S./Forms/C. 2118.

Army Form C. 2118

WAR DIARY
or
INTELLIGENCE SUMMARY

(Erase heading not required.)

VOLUME VI

SECRET

136 FIELD AMBULANCE

MAP REF. FRANCE 1/100000 ABBEVILLE

Instructions regarding War Diaries and Intelligence Summaries are contained in F. S. Regs., Part II. and the Staff Manual respectively. Title Pages will be prepared in manuscript.

Place	Date	Hour	Summary of Events and Information	Remarks and references to Appendices
VAUCHELLES-LE-QUESNOY	28/11/16	9 a.m.	Remaining Officers nil O.R. 13	Signed Griffith. Capt RAMC
	29/11/16	"	Remaining Officers nil O.R. 12	O.C.
	30/11/16	"	Remaining Officers nil O.R. 13	O.C.

Signed Griffith
Capt R.AMC
O C 136 F.A.

149/90

40th D⁰

136th Field Ambulance

Dec. 1916

COMMITTEE FOR THE
MEDICAL HISTORY OF THE WAR
Date 31 JAN. 1917

Army Form C.2118

WAR DIARY of 136 Field Ambulance H.Q. Division

INTELLIGENCE SUMMARY

(Erase heading not required.)

Vol. VII

Vol. VII   1st FIELD AMBULANCE 40th Divn   MAP REFERENCE 1/100,000 ABBEVILLE

Place	Date	Hour	Summary of Events and Information	Remarks and references to Appendices
VAUCHELLES-LE-QUESNOY	1-XII-16	9.00 a.m.	Remaining, Officers nil, O.R. 17	
	2-XII-16	"	" " nil, O.R. 23	
	3-XII-16	"	" " nil, O.R. 31	
	4-XII-16	"	" " nil, O.R. 18	
	5-XII-16	"	" " nil, O.R. 31	
	6-XII-16	"	" " nil, O.R. 32	
	7-XII-16	"	" " nil, O.R. 24	
	8-XII-16	"	" " 1, O.R. 27. Under orders from 119 Infantry Brigade, the Transport of the unit, except the motor ambulance cars, moved off by route of march at 1.30 p.m. to AILLY-LE-HAUT-CLOCHER, Captain T.H. HOUSTON R.A.M.C. in command.	
	9-12-16	"	Remaining, Officers nil, O.R. nil. Lieut-Col F.E. ROWAN-ROBINSON R.A.M.C. returned from leave to ENGLAND and assumed charge of the unit	
Camp 12 K.33.b	10.12.16	"	Under instructions from 119th Infantry Brigade the Unit Graco-Suffolk Capt Q.A. R.M.C. SR at 10 a.m – Entrained at EDGE HILL and Marched to PONT REMY to take Train to ALBERT Combined Sheet Camp 12. (K. 33 b.) where being arrived at 5.30 p.m. The journey was a long one, and the train somewhat took much an arrived at the Camp Offica Commdn Osis 1st R. at	

G.F. Rowan-Robinson
Lt Col RAMC

Army Form C.2118

WAR DIARY
or
INTELLIGENCE SUMMARY

1/136 Field Ambulance
40th Division
Army of France
ALBERT Command Sheet 1/40,000

Vol. VII

(Erase heading not required.)

Place	Date	Hour	Summary of Events and Information	Remarks and references to Appendices
CAMP 12 K 33 L	11.12.16	9am	Officers remaining. Out O.R. 1. The Camp was in a very insanitary state, the ground had been found with human excreta, its latrines had not been filled in, and refuse was lying about everywhere. Two sections of the ambulance were put to work to clean up the area occupied by the Field Ambulance. YPCR	
"	12.12.16		Officers Remain. Out O.R. 8. YPCR The work of cleaning up the camp and making paths was continued. YPCR	
"	13.12.16		Officers Remaining Out O.R. 14 YPCR	
"	14.12.16		Officers Remaining Out O.R. 24. YPCR The work of cleaning, pitting & being continued, and platform are being built under supervision of the R.E. YPCR	
"	15.12.16		Officers Remaining Out O.R. 25 YPCR	
"	16.12.16		" " Out O.R. 21 CAPT. GOSS detailed for duty with 12th K.O.R.L. YPCR	
"	17.12.16		" " " O.R. 22 CAPT. MORRIS detailed for duty with S W Borderers batchwork YPCR	
"	18.12.16		" " " O.R. 26 YPCR	
"	19.12.16		" " " O.R. 33 YPCR	
"	20.12.16		" " " O.R. 38 YPCR	
"	21.12.16		" " " O.R. 41 YPCR CAPT. HOUSTON detailed for duty with the 40th Division Work Bn. YPCR	

WAR DIARY or INTELLIGENCE SUMMARY

Army Form C.2118

136 Field Ambulance
Vol VII

ALBERT (continued) Sheet 57 d.5.000

Place	Date	Hour	Summary of Events and Information	Remarks and references to Appendices
Camp 12 R.33.b	22.12.16		Officer Personnel 3 O.R. 37. Under instruction from A.D.M.S. 40th Division proceeded to Army 17 C.8.6.9.9 to meet the O.C. 101st Field Ambulance with a view to taking over the duties of that Ambulance. At Camp 14 there is a large hut used as a temporary Rest Station. Accommodation for about 180 cases. The accommodation for men consists of one hut where they slept, and have their meals — no special accommodation for sergeants. The officers of the Field Ambulance and the A.Dn Staff are also in the same hut. There is a mess hut for the officers mess and sleeping quarters. After leaving Camp 14, proceeded to MAUREPAS (B.14.b) where there is accommodation for 20 beds, who are held in reserve in case they are required at the A.D.S. at LE PRIEZ FARM (B.6.a.4.1). Sister went to the A.D.S. at LE PRIEZ FARM. Accommodation for flying doom cases (during an emergency 60 cases have been accommodated — all sitting cases). There is also accommodation for 300.R and 3 officers from the trench pieces or officers. There is no accommodation for patients in the advanced Bear Post. C.7.6.9.8. When the Field Ambulance takes over it will be on stretcher hand over the cases to the bearers of COMBLES, they are then placed or carried on R to the hut C.10.32 on the road to the A.D.S. at LE PRIEZ FARM, R.P.Q.R. Stretchers and caters to the O.R. 39	
"	23.12.16		Officers Personnel 2 O.R. 97	
"	24.12.16		Officer Personnel 2 O.R. Parade served to C.O.S. Y.P.R.	

WAR DIARY or **INTELLIGENCE SUMMARY**

1/136 Field Ambulance 40th Division
ALBERT Combined Rest 1/0,000

Army Form C. 2118

Volume VII

Place	Date	Hour	Summary of Events and Information	Remarks and references to Appendices
Camp 12 K 33 b	25.12.16		Officers remaining 1. O.R. 11.	
		7.30 am	An advance party consisting of 2 officers and 22 O.R proceeded to LE PRIEZ FARM taking with them a water cart and a G.S. Wagon of 2 Uniforms. On the way the R.C.O's were left at Camp 19 and 1 R.C.O was. man at MAUREPAS (B 146) as holding parties. The remainder of the unit spent the day halting for supper and clearing up the bivouacs preparatory to moving the following morning. J/R.O. Camp preparatory to moving the following morning. J/R.O. Officers remaining 1. O.R. 2. The Unit marched at 7.30 am to Camp 17 arriving at 11.45 am. J/R.O.	
"	26.12.16			
Camp 17	27.12.16		Officers remaining 2 O.R. 5. Joined up the line to further investigate the arrangements for evacuating Officers wounded in the Left Retraction front that there was no accommodation for the sick & wounded at the Advanced R.P.(C.7.6.9.8) I have recommended letters at the R.A.P, or at the Advanced C.R.A.D.S. This could be sent a support to make as soon as possible at a point near August to make as soon as possible at a point near a R.A.P and an Advanced Bearer Post. J/R.O as a R.A.P and an Advanced Bearer Post. J/R.O.	
"	28.12.16		Remaining Officers in'l. D.R.Y. the same duties of the Country the line is slightly occupied water. J/R.O	
"	29.12.16		Remaining Officers and O.R.s. J/R.O	
"	30.12.16		Remaining Officers in'l O.R and J/R.O. for to prevent him were not be any admission to this if any	
"	31.12.16		Remaining Officers in'l and O.Rs. from the him were after Volume VIII F.J. Roberston A Scheme of evacuation from the him were after Volume VIII F.J. Roberston Lt. HEWITT attached for temporary duty took O" Suffolks to day. Lt. Col. Crane	

136th Field Ambulance

COMMITTEE FOR THE
MEDICAL HISTORY OF THE WAR
Date 13 MAR. 1917

WAR DIARY or INTELLIGENCE SUMMARY

Army Form C. 2118

Army VIII Corps — 136 Field Ambulance — 40th Division
ALBERT. Continue Sheet 40,000 Vol 8

Place	Date	Hour	Summary of Events and Information	Remarks and references to Appendices
Camp 14 K35c 986	1.1.17		There are at present no admissions to this Field Ambulance. All cars loaded through the A.D.S at LE PRIEZ FARM are shown as admissions at the Motor Dressing Station at MARICOURT. Corps Main Dressing Station of Lgt Bar Section 40th Division. Scheme of Evacuation of Lgt Bar Section of Rgt.Pk. R.A.P. C.17.b.9.3. Bn Hq R.A.P. on dug out — no accommodation for wounded. Connected by BAPAUME-PERONNE Road out by a recently constructed route along the western edge of this road with the left Bn.Hq R.A.P. advanced Plymouth Trench — about 180 yards. Plymouth Trench hand carry cars from the front line partly by trench & partly in the open over R.Bn.Hq to the A.B.P. C.1.a.8.1. Cars on the hard over to the brow of the hill via R.Bn.Hq to the A.B.P. C.1.a.8.1. Cars on the hard over to the brow of the hill Field Ambulance who carry them by Shelters by Trench to a point where the trench open on the COMBLES ROAD C.1.c.4.2 cars are then placed on wheeled stretchers and Later to LE PRIEZ FARM a distance of 800 yards from which stretchers are kept at the house C.1.c.4.2 on the COMBLES ROAD. Bn Hq W.7. BAPAUME PEPONNE Ra Left Bn. Bn Hq R.A.P. & A.B.P.C.1.a.8.1. Has accommodation with difficulty for an Ops R.A.P. - A.B.P. E. of the Road The R.A.P. has advanced because of the Case. A Shelter is being constructed next to the R.A.P. for the front line party to accommodate 10 men. Cars are brought from the front line partly. The Field Ambulance, partly in the open to the Left Bn R.A.P. & A.B.P and then carried by the R.Bn. by hand and partly in the open to the Left Bn R.A.P. & A.B.P and then carried by the R.Bn. & has been as described for the R.Bn.	

WAR DIARY / INTELLIGENCE SUMMARY

Army Form C. 2118

1/1st 86 Field Ambulance
4th Division
ALBERT Confirmed Sheet
1:5000

Place	Date	Hour	Summary of Events and Information	Remarks and references to Appendices
Camp 14.	1.1.17		Evacuation Scheme continued. Advanced Dressing Station LE PRIEZ FARM B6a3.2. On the other of which was a farm. Accommodation 20 lying cases. A number possibly 50 sitting & walking cases could be accommodated in neighbouring dug outs. Accommodation for personnel 3 Officers 30 O.R. You can see up to the road by the dressing station. All cars are evacuated in the order of this Field Amb to the 65th Indian Dressing as MARICOURT. Evacuation carried out by day & by night. Rescue Bearer Post MAUREPAS (B11b) Accommodation for 20 bearers. Three bearers are kept in reserve in case ambulance is required at the A.D.S.	
Camp 14.	2.1.17		Staff walking is being implemented with the Motor cars of the Ambulance. Dressing down and treatment there is only one in use. Horse ambulances are being sent up daily to assist with the evacuation.	
	3.1.17		Joined the A.D.S and convoyed them to the Depot. Lt. SINCLAIR reports his arrival for duty with this Unit. Year.	
	4.1.17		Another bearer post is being established at C.12.d.9. A walking party is sent up daily from the Reserve Bearer Post at MAUREPAS for the purpose.	

3 Secret

Army Form C. 2118

WAR DIARY
or
INTELLIGENCE SUMMARY
(Erase heading not required.)

136 Field Ambulance
10th Div.

Oct VIII

ALBERT (contd) Sheet

Place	Date	Hour	Summary of Events and Information	Remarks and references to Appendices
Camp 14	5.1.17		Lt. HEWITT rejoined the Unit to day. YSER BROR	
"	6.1.17		Capt. G. MORRIS rejoined the unit. 1st Div. BROR	
"	7.1.17		Capt. McCARTER detailed for temporary duty as D.O. to 18th Welch. Visited the A.D.S. and Transport lines for the inspection of horses.	
"	8.1.17		Visited the A.D.S. and A.B.P. YSER	
	9.1.17		Adm: inspect horses	
	10.1.17		Visited A.D.S. and A.B.P. Arrived at the A.D.S for the habit. YSER	
	11.1.17		Returned from A.D.S. YSER	
	12.1.17			
	13.1.17		Capt. R.C. CARTER returned from duty with 18th Welch. CAPT. GOSS attached as replacement M.O. to H.Q.R.L from 13th-19th inst. CAPT. MORRIS proceeded to LE BRIEZ FARM YSER Church Parade Services	
	14.1.17		Lt. HEWITT detailed for duty with H.L.I. A.D.M.S & D.A.D.M.S. visited A.D.S. at LE BRIEZ FARM YSER	
	15.1.17			
	16.1.17		Jam Buoy sent to C.C.S. to day suffering from P.U.O. Capt. Godfrey was taken over charge during any absence	
	17.1.17			

[signature]
O.C. F.A.

SECRET

4 136 FIELD AMBULANCE Army Form C. 2118
    40th DIV

WAR DIARY
or
INTELLIGENCE SUMMARY

(Erase heading not required.) MAP REF 1/40000 ALBERT combined sheet

Instructions regarding War Diaries and Intelligence Vol viii
Summaries are contained in F.S. Regs., Part II.
and the Staff Manual respectively. Title Pages
will be prepared in manuscript.

Place	Date	Hour	Summary of Events and Information	Remarks and references to Appendices
Bécourt G.8.c.	17-1-17	6 p.m.	Returned to HQ from A.D.S. LE PRIEZ and assumed command of the unit under orders from A.D.M.S. 40 Div.	Beaucourt-sur-Ancre Camp Ravine
	18-1-17		Captain R H PALMER R.A.M.C. reported his arrival from the sanitary camp & is taken on strength of the unit whilst W/ Hébert away during the tour on the line.	
	19-1-17		Lieut. & Q.M. H PULLAN reports his arrival from ENGLAND & is taken on the strength of the unit.	
	20-1-17		All motor ambulance cars running. 1 Secretary Daisy & 1 Ford car doubtful. Two 3D cars running cars running. 1 Secretary Daisy car struck by shell June GJ	
	21-1-17		Received from 137 Field Ambulance E. Col Sudbury Daisy car struck by shell June GJ	
			Visited the A.D.S. LE PRIEZ with Lt.Q.M. PULLAN. Bungalows & new relay beam just complete & still erecting shelters ready to put in position GJ	
	22-1-17		Visited by A.D.M.S. 40 Div. GJ	
	23-1-17		Visited by A.D.M.S. 8th Div. GJ	
	24-1-17		Visited by D.A.D.M.S. 40 Div. GJ	
	25-1-17		In conformity with O.C. 25 F.A. proceeded to LE PRIEZ FARM for tour of inspection, preparatory to relief of the unit by 25 F.A. new relay beam just complete & ready for occupation. GJ	
	26-1-17		Capt F manno helium a from A.D.S. Advanced party for billeting sent to new area GJ	
	27-1-17		Capt F.B. McCrea returned from A.D.S. having handed over A.D.S., A.D.P. & R.B.P. to 25 F.A. Report of work done during tour in the line, see appendix GJ	Appendix 1
	29-1-17		Handed over quarters in camp 19 to 25 F.A. Unit moved at 11 a.m. by motor lorry to SAILLY LAURETTE J.36 d. 4.3	

SECRET

Army Form C. 2118

136 Field Ambulance
40th Div.

WAR DIARY
or
INTELLIGENCE SUMMARY

(Erase heading not required.) MAP REF. 1-40,000 ALBERT combined sheet

Vol VIII

Place	Date	Hour	Summary of Events and Information	Remarks and references to Appendices
SAILLY-LAURETTE J36d.8.3	29-1-17	6 p.m.	Remaining Officers 2. O.R. 5. Visited A.D.M.S. 40 Div. re baths for 119 Bde.	
	30-1-17	do	Inspected bath-house in process of construction. Remaining Officers 2. O.R. 13.	
	31-1-17	do	Remaining Officers 2. O.R. 9. R.E. officer unable to refuse to bring baths into use, but temporary measures to be taken to complete at present on account of frost.	

Ricard Gapplelon
Capt Raine S.R.
O.C. 136 F.A.

Appendix to War Diary of 136 F.A. VOL VIII

SECRET

Report on Work done in RANCOURT Sector by 136 F.A.
25-12-16 to 23-1-17

On taking over the A.D.S. at LE PRIEZ Fm. it was found that the accommodation for bearers at the R.A.P. of the right B?. was non existent. The sanitary arrangements at LE PRIEZ consisted of an old and well used French latrine and that improvements were urgently required at the A.D.S. both in its structure & fittings. As a temporary measure, the construction of a shelter was at once taken in hand, at A??LLO accommodation being provided for two Bearer squads, & the shelter well sand bagged. A new deep pit latrine was dug at LE PRIEZ Fm. and the old one filled in. A new rack to take 9 stretcher cases was constructed on the A.D.S. The latrine was strutted where it showed signs of falling in, and the rain water tank of the farm, now dry, was cleaned out & made habitable. A report was sent in to A.D.M.S. and an R.E. officer was sent to report on improvements required in existing arrangements. It was decided to construct a new combined R.A.P. to serve both Right & Left B?. & an advanced Bearer Post. at A?LLO O.P.d.P.O.

at the new Bd H.Q., large enough to accommodate both R.M.O.'s and bearers & 12 lying cases. This was to be constructed by the R.E. At the same time, 136 F.A. started work on a relay bearer post at ABERDEEN. C.1.c.5.2. This will hold 12 lying cases & is proof against shells up to 5.9 calibre. It is roofed with steel cupolas & sand bags, & has one entrance into ABODE LANE & one to the road. Size 18 ft by 10 ft.

Both these dug-outs were completed on 25-1-17.

A further dug-out was cleaned out drained, & floored, to provide further accommodation at A.D.S. The officers accommodation at A.D.S. was improved and provision made for emergency accommodation for officers.

All these were completed before leaving the sector

PJacob Griffith
Capt RAMC
O.C. 136 F.A.

27/1/17

Copy no 1 - ADMS 40 Div
2 - war diary
3 - File.

140/1917

40 F. Amb.

136th Field Ambulance

COMMITTEE FOR THE
MEDICAL HISTORY OF THE WAR
Date 4 - APR. 1917

Volume IX   SECRET   136 Field Ambulance   Army Form C. 2118
                                        40th Division

WAR DIARY
or
INTELLIGENCE SUMMARY
(Erase heading not required.)   MAP REF 1/40000 ALBERT (covering sheet) Vol 9

Place	Date	Hour	Summary of Events and Information	Remarks and references to Appendices
SAILLY LAURETTE	1-2-17	6 p.m.	Baths at SAILLY LAURETTE put in working order by RE and taken over.	
136 a.3.3	2-2-17	—	Remaining Officers 2. O.R. 7. Ophthalmoplegia Capt Reid SR	
"	3-2-17	—	Remaining Officers 2. O.R. 11. Baths in use. about 300 men passed through. JR	
"	4-2-17	—	Remaining Officers and O.R. 14. JR	
"	5-2-17	—	Visited by A.D.M.S. 40th Division. Remaining Officers 2. O.R. 15. JR	
"	6-2-17	—	Remaining Officers 2. O.R. 18. Further billets found for personnel & dressing accommodation increased. JR	
"	7-2-17	—	Visited by DADMS 40th Div. Remaining Officers 1. O.R. 14. JR	
"	8-2-17	—	Remaining Officers 1. O.R. 18. JR	
"	9-2-17	—	Remaining Officers 1. O.R. 22. Lieut-Col F.E. ROWAN-ROBINSON returned from 3 weeks Officers Rest Station, and assumed command of the unit. Ophthalmoplegia Capt Burne SR 300 men of 119 Brigade had their feet washed with complete set of foot-powder - See French method. F.E. Rowan Robinson Lt Col RAMC	
"	10-2-17		Remaining Officers 1. O.R. 22	

Army Form C. 2118

130 Field Ambulance
L.O.L.Davy
Near ALBERT (Corbie Sheet) LS005

WAR DIARY
or
INTELLIGENCE SUMMARY

(Erase heading not required.)

Secret
Volume IX

Instructions regarding War Diaries and Intelligence Summaries are contained in F.S. Regs., Part II. and the Staff Manual respectively. Title Pages will be prepared in manuscript.

Place	Date	Hour	Summary of Events and Information	Remarks and references to Appendices
Camp 21 G30.9.9	10.2.17	8am	Two Tent Subdivisions proceeded to the XV Corps Vent Station for duty	
		9am	An advance party consisting of 1 Officer & 30 O.R. proceeded to Camp 21 to take over the duties of 26th Field Ambulance. The main convoy of personnel & stores later to consist the load side Consisting to carry out the French custom of prevention of frozen feet and of attacks wings of the Bath. The Baths were out of use owing to the frost having frozen the boilers. The Baths were out of use and the camp water supply was frozen up. B.R.R. and some of the pipes	
	11.2.17		Reinforcing Officer Oil I.R. 10 The main body marched to Camp 21 B.R.R.	
	12.2.17		Reinforcing Officer Ind O.R. 1 the day Lt.G.A. Brent in hospital his Destiny Platoon who had left for the post-Baths. B.R.R.	
	13.2.17		Reinforcing Officer Ind O.R. 26 B.R.R.	
	14.2.17		Reinforcing Officer Ind O.R. 91. 1st D.A.H. MOSES reported for duty. B.R.R.	
	15.2.17		Reinforcing Officer Ind O.R. 20 B.R.R.	
	16.2.17		Reinforcing Officer Ind O.R. 19 The Field Ambulance Troupe gave a performance in the Church army hut during the evening. B.R.R.	
	17.2.17		Reinforcing Officer I.R. 17 Cpl GOSS detailed for permanent duty with 12th Suffolks B.R.R.	

Army Form C. 2118

WAR DIARY
or
INTELLIGENCE SUMMARY
(Erase heading not required.)

Secret
Volume IX

136 Field Ambulance
R.A.M.C.
H.Q. Rd. ALBERT (communicated road)

Instructions regarding War Diaries and Intelligence Summaries are contained in F. S. Regs., Part II. and the Staff Manual respectively. Title Pages will be prepared in manuscript.

Place	Date	Hour	Summary of Events and Information	Remarks and references to Appendices
Camp XI BG3a98	18.2.17		Remains officers lid. O.R. 18 Capt MORRIS detailed for water supply duties with 11th H.L.I. 4 O.R.	
"	19.2.17		Remains officers lid. O.R 16 Capt BUCK M CARTER detailed for permanent duty with 11th H.L.I. 4 O.R.	
"	20.2.17		Remains officers lid 8 O.R.14 Capt MORRIS detailed for permanent duty with 8 W.B. 4 O.R.	
"	21.2.17		Remains officers 3 O.R 25 2nd Lt HEWITT having been transferred to Trench 1/1 H.O. struck off 4 O.R.	
"	22.2.17		Remains officers 3 O.R 6 4 O.R.	
"	23.2.17		Remains officers 2 O.R 28 4 O.R.	
"	24.2.17		Remains officers 2 O.R 91 4 O.R.	
"	25.2.17		Remains officers 3 R 17 4 O.R.	
"	26.2.17		Capt RICHARDSON at present sick on leave to the unit on duty 4 O.R.	
"	27.2.17		Remains officers 1 O.R 17 4 O.R.S	
"	28.2.17		Remains officers 4 O.R 6 R 28	

[signature]
Lt Col
Comdg 136 F Amb

40/1086

40 V Res

136.1. 7. A.

COMMITTEE FOR THE
MEDICAL HISTORY OF THE WAR
Date ≡ 6 JUN. 1917

Army Form C. 2118

Volume X Scott

136 Field Ambulance H.Q.
(O.C. Lt J ALBERT (returned sick))
Vol 10

WAR DIARY
or
INTELLIGENCE SUMMARY
(Erase heading not required.)

Instructions regarding War Diaries and Intelligence Summaries are contained in F.S. Regs., Part II. and the Staff Manual respectively. Title Pages will be prepared in manuscript.

Place	Date	Hour	Summary of Events and Information	Remarks and references to Appendices
Camp 21 C3a 98	1/3/17		Remains Office huts O.R. 24. 4 Platoons and Stretchers at Le Ram-	
"	2/3/17		Football drawn 4-4 11th O.R.L. Remains Office huts O.R. 27. Football 1. 13th E. Surrey Regt. Remains Office huts O.R.21. ADMS	
"	3/3/17		Remains Office huts O.R. 20	
"	4/3/17		Football 1 - 11th 110 R.L. v Bn E Surrey Regt	
"	5/3/17		Ambulances of 50 bearers instructions on tents to be attached to the 25th Field Ambulance. Their roles were in relieve for the 8th Division. Remains Office huts O.R. 19. Bearer party delivered to Headquarters of Divisional H.Q.R	
"	6/3/17		Office Remains huts O.R. 14. Bell (foot) L. 19 R.W.Y. v 15th Worth R.R.	
"	7/3/17		Remains Office huts O.R.3 Lovie	
"	8/3/17		Remains Office huts O.R. huts F.W.R.	
Suzanne C8d9.2	9/3/17		Remains huts 1 O.R.41. The Unit marched to Suzanne and took over the duties of 101st Field Ambulance and to attend to sick at Curlu area	
"	10/3/17		Remains Office huts 1 O.R. 51 Hosp.	

Army Form C. 2118

WAR DIARY
or
INTELLIGENCE SUMMARY
(Erase heading not required.)

Volume X

136 Field Ambulance
110th Division
Sheet
was at ALBERT continued Sheet
No. 0,000

Instructions regarding War Diaries and Intelligence Summaries are contained in F. S. Regs., Part II. and the Staff Manual respectively. Title Pages will be prepared in manuscript.

Place	Date	Hour	Summary of Events and Information	Remarks and references to Appendices
SUZANNE CBA2	11.3.17		Remaining Officers 1 OR 54 free	
"	12.3.17		Remaining Officers 1 OR 55. CAPT HEWITT & CAPT RUTHERFORD reported to Coln Winn for duty free	
"	13.3.17		Remaining Officers 1 OR 18 free	
"	14.3.17		Remaining Officers 1 OR 47 free	
"	15.3.17		Remaining Officers 1 OR 62 free. The last to under orders to open at Chene Walwin	
"	16.3.17		Remaining Officers 1 OR 40 free	
"	17.3.17		Remaining Officers 1 OR 37. The Ambulance Commr opened an Information at the SUZANNE theatre free	
"	18.3.17		Remaining Officers 1 OR 34 free	
"	19.3.17		Remaining Officers 1, OR 29 free	
"	20.3.17		Remaining Officers 1. OR 21 free	
HEM H8a	21.3.17		Remaining Officers 1 OR fee free. CAPT RUTHERFORD detailed for temporary duty with 196 RAY. CAPT RICHARDSON reported for duty. The Unit proceeded to HEM during the Officer and 12 O.R. to hold the bitten - hostilities at SUZANNE and a bearer to continue running the talk at CURLU free	
"	22.3.17		Remaining Officers 1. OR 4. Capt HENRY Hallwell for temporary duty with 10th W. Div. A.C. CAPT RICHARDSON proceeded to HAUTEALLAINES for duty with a Mobile Column. A bearer sub-division in chg of Capt. GAFFIKIN free	

1875 Wt. W593/826 1,000,000 4/15 J.B.C. & A. A.D.S.S./Forms/C. 2118.

WAR DIARY
or
INTELLIGENCE SUMMARY

(Erase heading not required.)

Army Form C. 2118

136 Field Ambulance
10th Division
Area of ALBERT contined Sheet

Place	Date	Hour	Summary of Events and Information	Remarks and references to Appendices
HEM	23.3.17		Remains Officers 1 O.R. 4. ¥R20	
"	24.3.17		Remains Officers 1 O.R. 1 ¥R22. An advanced dressing Station has been opened at CHERY HECOURT. ¥R22	
"	25.3.17		Remains Officers 1 O.R. 6 ¥R22. The team Rendezvous where the Motor teleow & the bearers allocated to 131 ¥Amb for duty returns to Headquarters at HEM to-day. ¥R22	
"	26.3.17		Remains Officers 1 O.R. 8 ¥R22	
"	27.3.17		Remains Officers 1 O.R. 16 ¥R22.	
"	28.3.17		Remains Officers 1 O.R. 12 ¥R22	
"	29.3.17		Remains Officers an O.R. 12 ¥R22. Lt. W. WORTHINGTON reported for duty with this unit. CAPT T.H. HOUSTON transferred to the Corps Main Dressing Station from	
"	30.3.17		Remains Officers an R. 6 R. 15. ¥R22	
"	31.3.17		Remains Officers an R. 6 R. 16. CAPT RICHARDSON attached for duty with 30th Ambulance temporarily.	

F.P.Bowman Lotyer
Lt Col R.AMC

COMMITTEE FOR THE
MEDICAL HISTORY OF THE WAR
Date —6 JUN.1917

136. F. A.

40th Div.

April 1917
S

Secret
Army Form C. 2118

WAR DIARY
or
INTELLIGENCE SUMMARY
(Erase heading not required.)

M 136 Field Ambulance
H.Q. "Division"
Map Reference France $\frac{62c}{57c}$ 1/40,000
Volume XI

Instructions regarding War Diaries and Intelligence Summaries are contained in F.S. Regs., Part II. and the Staff Manual respectively. Title Pages will be prepared in manuscript.

Place	Date	Hour	Summary of Events and Information	Remarks and references to Appendices
HEM H 8a	April 1st 1917		Reconnoitring Officers in O.R. 16. Patrols and Returns 1st & 2nd Division	
"	2nd		Remaining Officers in O.R. 11. Under instruction from O.D.M.S. 116th Div. Invested MANANCOURT V.13 ETRICOURT V.8 EQUANCOURT V.10 and FINS V.12 for the purpose of finding suitable building for a dressing station and to find rooms suitable for the separation of sick & wounded CAPT RUTHERFORD returned from duty with 1/4 R.W.F. YSER	
"	3rd		Remaining Officers in O.R. 2. Remaining Officer in O.R. 2	
"	4th		Remaining Officers in O.R. 2	
"	5th		An advance party of one Officer & after O.R. proceeded to MANANCOURT for the purpose of holding suitable buildings for a Dressing Station.	
"	6th		Remaining Officers in O.R. One The main body of the unit marched HEM to MOISLAINS C.18a and billeted there for the night. 1 NCO	
"			Remaining Officers in O.R. One Unit marched from MOISLAINS & MANANCOURT V.13 and commenced receiving	
MANANCOURT V.13	7th		a left States as an advance party. Then 1 officer and J.6 O.R. proceeded to FINS V.12 to form an Advanced Dressing Station Inside the information left posts on this line. Captain RUTHERFORD refer unit touch with 119th Brigade HQ a... the munition...	

Secret

Army Form C. 2118

WAR DIARY
or
INTELLIGENCE SUMMARY

(Erase heading not required.)

Of 1/36 Field Ambulance
10th Division
6?03 140 000
Lieut Col Frazer

Volume XI

Place	Date	Hour	Summary of Events and Information	Remarks and references to Appendices
MANANCOURT	April 8		Remain officer i/o R.A.P. CAPT A.S. SMITH reported for duty with this unit. Method of evacuation from the present front line of 1/10th Division. R.A.P. of 1/4 Lt. B. is situated at S.W. entrance of DESSART WOOD at W.2.C.9.9. R.A.P. of Right Bn is situated at E end of DESSART WOOD at FINS. Horse ambulances and Motor Ambulances can be driven along the advanced dressing station in shelter at COUZEAUCOURT road as far as the advanced dressing station road at W.2.C.6.5. on the side the line road by the bearers of the F. Amb from the R.A.P.'s brought there road wack in Cars and Feet to the Advanced dressing Station at FINS. At FINS there is accommodation for 20 patients. The personnel consists of 1 Officer & 26 O.R. from FINS cases are evacuated in motor cars direct to the C.M.D.S. at MARICOURT via NURLU- MOISLAINS - CLERY. Slightly wounded & sick to the dressing Station at MANANCOURT. At MANANCOURT there is accommodation for 100 cases. Evacuation from the dressing station are sent to the C.M.D.S. at MARICOURT. The cars of 137 Field Ambulance assist in evacuating these cases. 137 Field Amb is stationed at MOISLAINS. BRR	
	9th		Remain officer i/o R.A.P. YPP CAPT RICHARDSON having been detailed for duty at 38 C.C.S. in similar of the unit. CAPT A.J.SMITH detailed for duty with 2nd Middlesex	

WAR DIARY or INTELLIGENCE SUMMARY

Army Form C. 2118

136 Field Ambulance 40th Division

Place	Date	Hour	Summary of Events and Information	Remarks and references to Appendices
MANANCOURT	April 10		Receiving Officer hit O.R. Not instructor. Wired from A.D.M.S. that I am to take over the duties of acting A.D.M.S. 40th Division and the command of the Field Ambulance to be handed over as possible to CAPT P. GAFFIKIN from as possible. CAPT P. GAFFIKIN took over an afternoon affording the work of the brems in the first line.	
"	April 11		Receiving Officer hit O.R. has On admission had discharge from is only light for cases without his hat. formed beyond the dressing station - Cases evacuated are shown as a their years at the Corps Main Dressing Station. J.D. Roro-Buckley Lt. Col. acting A.D.M.S. 40 Div handed over to P.E. ROWAN ROBINSON RAMC R. established Capt R.A.M.C. 38. acting A.D.M.S. 88	
April 12	6 p.m.	Assumed command of this unit I am lent Col to 88 Receiving officers not O.R. nil.	
April 12	"	Visited A.D.S. and advanced Bearer posts in company with acting A.D.M.S. 88	
April 13	"	Receiving officers not O.R. nil 88	
April 14	"	Visited A.D.S. advanced bearer posts and regimental aid posts Receiving officers not O.R. nil 88	
April 15	"	Receiving officers not O.R. nil 88	
April 16	"	Visited A.D.S. advanced bearer posts & R.A.P.'s & arrangement made for evacuation	

Army Form C. 2118

WAR DIARY or INTELLIGENCE SUMMARY

(Erase heading not required.)

136 Field Ambulance

VOL XI

SECRET

Instructions regarding War Diaries and Intelligence Summaries are contained in F.S. Regs., Part II. and the Staff Manual respectively. Title Pages will be prepared in manuscript.

Place	Date	Hour	Summary of Events and Information	Remarks and references to Appendices
MANANCOURT	April 16 1917 (Mon)	6 pm	MAP REF. 1/20000 FRANCE 62c & 57c. One site for advanced dressing posts in METZ & GOUZEAUCOURT areas, in company with A/ADMS 4/0 E Div. Reviewing Officers not OR nil Off	
	April 17		Capt. MOHAN R.A.M.C. (T.C.) reported for duty. Officers Reviewing not OR nil Off	
	" 18		Visited H.Q. 120 Inf Bde with A.D.M.S. Reviewing officers nil OR nil Off	
	" 19		Visited A.D.S. & A.D.Ps. Visited H.Q. 119 Inf. Bde Captain H.S. BERRY R.A.M.C. (T.C.) reported for duty. Lieut-Col F.E. ROWAN-ROBINSON returned from H.Q. 40th Div & re-assumed command of the unit Reviewing officers nil OR nil & re-assumed command	
			Signed Rowan Robinson Capt. R.A.M.C. S.R.	
	" 20		Arrangements from made to the supply of casualties early to advanced dressing. The present evacuation return is as follows. The R.A.P. of the R.B. (13th York) consists of a bell tent situated at W 2.d.2.6. R.A.P. of the J.R. (21 Middlesex) consists of a dug out shelter at the S.W. extremity of DESSART WOOD with a Bearer Post in front made at the side of the FINS-GOUZEAUCOURT ROAD at W76.8.8. Advanced Dressing Station at FINS V12.C.5.4. Apart from last accommodation for ... patients. Present 1 officer 20 O.R. Transport two horse ambulance. Donkeylounts sent from Units with the 121 Brigade and the regiments in the line to Revelon then taken to front to the A.D.S. at FINS when an ambulance is required	

1875. Wt. W593/826 2,000,000. 4/15 J.B.C. & A. A.D.S.S./Forms/C. 2118.

Army Form C. 2118

WAR DIARY
or
INTELLIGENCE SUMMARY
(Erase heading not required.)

Vol XI Secret
136 F Ambulance BDW Brie
MAP ref France 1:10,000 57 c 62

Place	Date 1917	Hour	Summary of Events and Information	Remarks and references to Appendices
MANANCOURT V.13	Apr 20th		From A.D.S. at FINS cases are evacuated in Motor Ambulances to the Dressing Station at MANANCOURT V.13.a.9.3 from the Dressing Station cases are evacuated by Motor Cars to MOISLAINS from the to the C.C.C.S. in the cars of 137 Field Ambulance HQ Péronne Péronne Pilon Place	
"	"	9 A	An attack was made by the 110th Division at 4.am this morning. Casualties commenced to arrive shortly after this hour. Position of R.a.P's were as follows. 19th R.W.F at Q.36 c 3-7 KD.R.h Q 31.68.2 19th S.W.B Q 30 a 9.9 Past Pursey Q 23 c 7.3 18th Welch Q 30 d 8.8 17 Welsh Queens Posts Beau Posts 1. at COUZEAUCOURT combined with R.a.P. of 19th R.W.F Q 36c.3.7 strong 2. Cross Road W 4 a 1.3 in a sunken road. 5 O.P.'s and a Bomb station under charge of Rev. MATTHIAS 3. Queens Cross Q 30 a 9.9 4. METZ in a cellar Q 25 d 1.9. 10. to 10 am. Late in the day there been horse drawn Ambulance attending to requirements. Wheeled evacuation at Beaucamps and at COUZEAUCOURT. Two hors cars cleared cases from METZ to FINS. Two horse Ambulances and Ford cleared cases from the 2 Beau Posts crossroad to FINS later in the day. As horse cars cleared cases from the Dr.S on the FINS COUZEAUCOURT ROAD at Q 35. A 2.2. As Ford cars cleared cars from the Dr.S. to be collected for from the R.A.E. To ascertain the number of cars not to be collected for from the R.A.E. From information it was possible to evacuate that the wounded From information obtained from as many quarters as possible it was ascertained that all wounded had been collected and cleared by 9.30 am. After the time only the normal casualties arrived the A.D.S. as a result of the engagement. Officers 22. O.R. 244 = 266 Hostel 3 289 R.B.W. P.M.P.	

Vol XI Scout.

Army Form C. 2118

136 Field Ambulance W.O.R. Summary

Map ref 1:10,000 62c.
57c.

WAR DIARY
or
INTELLIGENCE SUMMARY

(Erase heading not required.)

Place	Date 1917	Hour	Summary of Events and Information	Remarks and references to Appendices
MANANCOURT	April 23		The situation became normal. The day was spent in improving the accommodation for patients at FINS. The Officer Commanding, at 10 o'clock sent the A.D.M.S. 20th to consult about arrangements for the evacuation of wounded the following day. The Division was to attack at 4 am on the 24th. It was decided that 136 F. Amb. should proceed to FINS at once, and 137 Field Amb. should proceed to MANANCOURT and take over from Rest Division of 137 Field Ambulance moved to Lieramont. Also for 136 F. Amb. At 2pm. Officer toured the forward posts of the F. Amb. and the R.A.P's of the Left Brigade. The O.C. of the Division gave instructions on the position on the day previous that instructions of the R.A.P.'s of the Right Brigade and but an officer of 136 F. Amb. to ascertain the position in the town. After consulting the two arranged to take in the town which will later. After arrangements which had been made of the Division and informed the A.D.M.S. of the arrangements which had been made. Headquarters of 136 Field Ambulance completed the move to FINS by 9pm. The bearer subdivision of 137 F. Amb. relieved the bearers of 136 F. Amb. who were drawn from the Left Brigade. This was completed by 2am. night of April 23/24. The bearers of 136 F. Amb. a/c being relieved proceeded to reinforce the bearers drawing from the Right Brigade. Evacuation scheme was as follows:- Right Brigade R.A.P. R.B. R25a3.9 (in a Quarry) R.A.P. L.B. R19a to FIFTEEN RAVINE A.D.S. at Q.c.8.6 in a dammed house in GOUZEAUCOURT. Personnel 2 Officers 160 OR. 4/100 horsed ambulances. One ford car to clear to dressing station at FINS.	

WAR DIARY or INTELLIGENCE SUMMARY

Army Form C. 2118

136 Field Amb. 40th Division

Vol XI Serial

Place	Date	Hour	Summary of Events and Information	Remarks and references to Appendices
FINS	April 23		Evacuation Scheme contd:- Bearer Posts situated as follows. Parties divided between stretchers Q 30 c 8 3 10 bearers R 19 a 8 3 4 " R 25 d 2 6 (Farm) 16 " Q 36 c 6 7. 16 Bearers to carry Cars across a large track in GOUZEAUCOURT. Left Brigade Right R.a.P. a field Q 22 a 1 8. 8 bearers to take these to A.D.S. When Stretcher Bns bearers and two wheeled stretcher units to A.D.S at METZ Q 20 2 30 Right R.a.P. R 13 central 8 bearers clear from here to Bn Hqr at Q 18 d 05 when there is a delay. Post of 1/8th & 9th bearers then ferried to relay post at Q 23 c 8 2 where there are 13 bearers. The latter carry to Q 28 d 33 QUEENS CROSS where there are 16 bearers and four wheeled stretchers. From there to Wajou Rendezvous and Crossroads Q 24 6 23 and then by wagon to A.D.S. A.D.S. has two horsed Ambulances and car for use at its disposal. Bearers gradually helped forward the arrangement therefore was not complete until the 24th April.	
	April 24		to the new alignment hour Advanced Cars in Contumacy all day. The transport of the Walking Wounded Guide continues with the busy number of casualties. There officers were dressed; farm containing all day and the walk continued. throughout the night. The A.D.S arranged for better transport to I.R.C. and proven lorries. Sufficient volunteer workers always available as soon as car were moved they loaded on two cars, or lorries and sent into C.A.D.S. In anticipation of an improvement a large Quantity of battle comforts and Clothing had been accumulated Plenty of carts were available all day. In addition to the food which was at FINS a field kitchen was in continuous use at the A.D.S. at Q 20112 GAUZEAUCOURT and at METZ	

WAR DIARY or INTELLIGENCE SUMMARY

Army Form C. 2118

Vol XI Part 136 F. Ambulance
A.D.S. Gouzeaucourt
Mar 1917 R.25/0 57c

Place	Date	Hour	Summary of Events and Information	Remarks and references to Appendices
FINS	April 24th		It was reported that our troops were repulsed. Another few prisoners of 137 Bde had been collected & were wounded from the left Brigade.	
"	25		11 OMEN to A.D.S. RE assist in bringing cars and general assistance including the German stretcher helpers in the loan of 7 Gerber Stretchers.	YRR
"			We took in to Mercury Hill 28 German patients who were lying around the end of tramway line. The A.D.S. at GOUZEAUCOURT was removed from this house which had been in use to a field at 6.36 central where it was protected by a bank.	
"			Capt. O.R. 75011 Pte Jones W.H. 137 Field Amb. injured 9.24/25. J. S. ARMISTEAD Qmmr went for duty with this Unit and in return on the transfer from this date.	
"	26th		By St. Cavalier were clear and the situation becoming normal. The Brigade had a trying time during the operation, the fatigue as soon as it is known that the Brigade is to take the line being Messed to be forward to forward as possible at the Railway Arsenal so that the line is an hour before this becomes dangerous.	Infantry 2:? 52.? to-day OR 5005 PO-R 2 5:50 R.O.O.officer 2 O.R. 97
			An appendix is included by O.R. A.D.S GOUZEAUCOURT R.A.P. at A.D.S. Below the Recession Station.	
			From 94 to 96 h.17 following were taken evacuated	
"	26th		The book of information accommodation for wounded contained.	
"	27th		Casualties of the Unit 69/65 Pte Rawcliffe W.J. 15/87 Pte Pooley R. 90012 Pte Beckett W. were killed by artillery	
"	28th		The firing on the night 27/28 h 1729 83/95 Pte Self C. 16148 Pte Whitley J. was wounded by the same shell	
"	29th		From Gerdulum 71/37/8 Amb Returned to Hers. 137 Ambb Y.R.R 2 Regt. Bearer Bearers 12 S.W. R. R.A.P. R.A.P 177 with loss one Officer Evac-ant of GOUZEAUCOURT R.A.P on Gouzecroix. 19 R.C & R.A.P
"	30		Reg Brigade R.A.P	
			in the supply Unit (Regt. 6 Bann. Bearers, 18 Britt Infantry Amb. R.A.P. followed by R.C.G.S.O Division Reserve: Railway front 9 platoon at R.25e50 follow up	

Appendix I. War Diary Vol XI

WAR DIARY
or
INTELLIGENCE SUMMARY

Army Form C. 2118

136 FIELD AMBULANCE
40 DIV

SECRET

App A

Place	Date	Hour	Summary of Events and Information	Remarks and references to Appendices
MAMMANCOURT U.10.78.2.	10/4/19	6 p.m.	Map Ref. FRANCE 57c.S.W. Sheet 57c. Operation on 9-10/4/19 in conjunction with attack by 21st Middlesex Regt. The advance by the infantry was initiated at 3 p.m. about 4 p.m. I made a reconnaissance and came up to B²H.Q. entered Rd. moved forward to Z. Lewielin now A.27c.74. Ours had not put come up to that time. Then I found that the R.M.O. tried to release & carry up the F.A. bearers several wounded cases. I advanced Then & rapidly of Mamange. On again reaching B².HQ. I brought up 6 stretcher squads into the R.M.O. did not come up. I decided to I found some further wounded. But there were further wounded on out part of the position to put up R.M.O. It was infeasible that they established to evacuate to ADS by 6 a.m. at 9 am. 9.28. 6.92. I was informed by scout I collected all the wounded were collected at shop all wounded were collected by scout. That all the to B². H.Q. & infantry to the A.D.S. & returned the F.A. bearers to the A.D.S.	

R Jacob Griffiths
Captain R.A.M.C. F.R.

Army Form C. 2118

WAR DIARY
or
INTELLIGENCE SUMMARY
(Erase heading not required.)

Army Form C. 2118

136 Field Ambulance
10th Division
Head of Column 69th Division

Place	Date	Hour	Summary of Events and Information	Remarks and references to Appendices
	25/9		The A.D.S. had the use of 2 Ford Motor Ambulances, and 2 horse ambulances. The existing caves were surrounded without delay by the Ford Cars, whilst the less serious sitting and walking cases were evacuated to the horse ambulances. Walking accommodation was provided for the cases, but the transport was considered to warrant to keep them. The D.D.M.S. visited the A.D.S. in the morning about 2 hours after your own visit. Reports were received from the bearer posts that the Bearer service was working satisfactorily. Right Brigade - 14th 19 R.W.F. in the line with Pre. Sqdn in Epleur Ravine about S 19 a 9.4. To — posted in support with Bn. HQ at S 19 a 5 4. Sept. 18th Welsh and 12 S.W.B. in the order. Bearers as follows: 8 Bearers to evacuate the Bn T Sept 14th " on S 25 C 9 t. went they made a post. Sept 8 Bearers for 18th Welsh on on 24th 8 Bearers & Carters at on 24th J.R.C.O. relieving S.B. for bearer work with ADS. Casualties much less than on previous day - 10th? 23 as follows: 19 Welsh - 12, 18th Welsh - 3, 19 R.W.F. - 1, 15 S.W.B. - 1, 12 R.W.F. - 1 Arrangements at A.D.S. same as on 24th. No difficulty in dealing with same.	App I
	26/9		As on 25th. 5 Casualties - 18th Welsh 1 = 5 } 2 Intercommunication 13 S.W.B = 3 = 2 19 to R.B = 1 = 9 19 R.W.F = 1 Bearers as on 25th. No difficulty in dealing with same. The position of A.D.S. in Gouzeaucourt, owing to proximity of another battery of guns, instability of building, and on the advice of Staff Officers reported to you, and with your permission, was transferred to Ridge 200 yds west of old A.D.S. on S. Side of Finn-Gouzeaucourt Road	

Appendix 2
Vol XI Scene

WAR DIARY
or
~~INTELLIGENCE~~ SUMMARY
(Erase heading not required.)

Army Form C. 2118

136 Field Ambulance
40th Division
Map of France 57c 1/40.000

Place	Date	Hour	Summary of Events and Information	Remarks and references to Appendices
			In anticipation of some advance and the Hd. Qrs. of Ambulance transferring from Manancourt to the Advanced Dressing Station at Fins, Capt. Berry and myself were instructed on the night of 23rd April to push forward to Gouzeaucourt to establish an Advanced Dressing Station at Gouzeaucourt at the old Reg. Aid Post, vacated by the 19th R.W.F. on the night of 21-4-17, which fortunately having in view a possible advance, had been held by our Ambulance with some equipment and an N.C.O. in charge. The detachment of 137 Field Ambulance at 3 am on the morning of 24th April, established themselves at Metz at our former Bearer post - relieved our N.C.O's and bearers, and from this time undertook the evacuation of wounded from the left Brigade, having on the left A.&S. Highldrs. with the 13th? in support, and on the right the [illegible], with the [illegible] in support.	
			The 136th Amb. with the bearers already posted for the work in the line, later supplemented by 2 N.C.O's and 16 bearers from Metz, with our Advanced Dressing Stn. in the building at the West Entrance to Gouzeaucourt in charge of Capt. Berry, R.A.M.C., and myself, undertook the evacuation of wounded from the Reg. Aid Posts from the R. Brigade, with left 17th Welsh in the line with Reg. Aid Posts at Q 30 d. [illegible], having in support 19 R.W.F. Right 18th Welsh in the line with Reg. Aid Post at R 25 d. 1.2 (in Quarry) having in support 12 S.W.B.	
			Bearers were as follows:- 16 bearers (R.A.M.C.) evacuating from the 17th Welsh R.A.P.	
			12 " & 1 N.C.O. do. " " " 18 " "	
			8 bearers do on a relay post at a cellar in Gouzeaucourt	
			1 N.C.O. supervising and patrolling between the A.D.S. the bearer posts & Reg. Aid Posts	
			The first wounded arrived at Gouzeaucourt about 4 am. 24th April, and came in steadily all day, totalling for the 24 hrs. 100 cases as follows:-	
			19 R.W.F. = 10, E. Surrey = 38, H.L.I. = 3, 17 Welsh = 40?, 18th Welsh = ?, 119 M.G.C. = 1, German = 4.	
			All the cases were re-dressed or splinted as occasion arose, and were given 500 units A.T.S. if wounded - also a kitchen was kept going, and the wounded supplied with food and hot stimulating drinks	

WAR DIARY
or
INTELLIGENCE SUMMARY

Army Form C. 2118

Vol XI. Appendix 2.

136 Field Amb
40th Divn
Sheet of France 57c.C.10 c.s.w

Place	Date	Hour	Summary of Events and Information	Remarks and references to Appendices
	27/4/17		As on 25th — Usual visits in the afternoon and tour of inspection of the Line. Casualties — Nil. Sick Evacuated { R.W.F. — 8 R.M.F. — 1 S.W.B. — 1 Yeoman — 1 } Events as on 25th., with Stretcher to Regt. Aid Post of 19 R.W.F. at Elzear Farm. Also one Bearer with each Sig. Sta. O. to act as runner.	

(Sgd.) R.W. Rutherford
Lieut R.A.M.C.

H.Rosecrans Johnson
Lt Col R.A.M.C.

May 1917

40th Div.

136th F.A.

140/2161

COMMITTEE FOR THE
MEDICAL HISTORY OF THE WAR
Date 10 JUL. 1917

WAR DIARY or INTELLIGENCE SUMMARY

Army Form C. 2118

Vol XII Secret   136 Field Ambulance   Vol 12
                  40th Division

Place	Date 1917	Hour	Summary of Events and Information	Remarks and references to Appendices
FINS	May 2nd		Received information that an attack would soon be made on LA VACQUERIE and was given instruction by the O.D.M.S. 40th Div. to investigate the roads so that all routes of evacuation could be made use of. The report of my investigation was 1. That the GOUZEAUCOURT - CAMBRAI road could not be made use of - it was covered from GOUZEAUCOURT because of that it was inadvisable to attempt evacuation through GOUZEAUCOURT because I was informed by Military Authorities that when an attack was made on LA VACQUERIE, GOUZEAUCOURT would be very heavily shelled and would use all available trench implements for Ambulances. 3. A cross country track had been made by the Transport of the Right Brigade for keeping up ration. This on the whole was very much suitable route for evacuation of wounded. The track began near the cuts roads at W.30.5.8 to QUEENS CROSS @ 28.m.3 the 500 yards along METZ-GOUZEAUCOURT R. towards GOUZEAUCOURT by cross country to A 30.6.52 on the TRESCAULT-GOUZEAUCOURT R. 100yds along the road and then by horse again to R.19.c.9.3 on the GOUZEAUCOURT VILLERS PLOUICH R. along the road as far as FIFTEEN RAVINE the further point to which ambulance can be put. It was decided to move the A.D.S. near GOUZEAUCOURT to a sunken road at Q.29 c 3.5.	
	May 3rd		The A.D.S. of the Division inspected the site and examined it further than. The O.D.S was moved to the new A.D.S. Field kitchen heavily shelled on its arrival there. Five heavy casualties amongst horse + men killed. The trans Any Wound D.D.M.S. to A.D.S.'s trip inspects the dressing station at FINS. ffrr	

2 Oct XII Sent

WAR DIARY or **INTELLIGENCE SUMMARY**
(Erase heading not required.)

Army Form C. 2118

136 Field Ambulance
10th Division
Vieux Ferme France 40 000 5/c

Place	Date 1917	Hour	Summary of Events and Information	Remarks and references to Appendices
FINS	Aug 5th		The ADS was again shelled today. Mr Shilles which had been constructed for shelter the wounded was destroyed. The O/C ADS went often to another shelter road close by at Q29 c 99. The attack began at 11h to-day. The attack was both on a large scale here this morning later. After the first line was to return to their original line keeping back tents but in it. After the first the troops were to return to their original line keeping back tents. Men all killed & wounded. Elevated casualties 2,500. Two Bearer Subdivisions from 137 Field Ambulance reinforced the Bearer of this Unit. All the Bearer posts in the line deserted and Bearers under Capt BERRY were left at the Quarry Q25 c 28. One hundred extra stretcher were sent up the line. Six of them were handed over to the Regimental Bearers as it appears from the number of the actions that the Regimental Bearers could not cope as they predicted as they could deal with. The bearer posts were situated at:- 1. FIFTEEN RAVINE Q19 c 41 2. SIXTEENTH RAVINE Q20 c 99 3. R 21 c 6.3 4. R 20 d 6.4. 5. Quarry R25 d 39 (Regimental Bearers at distant of Bearer Affairs) 6. Q30 b 5.4 (Relay Port) The number of Bearers at their posts being continually according to the requirements of the R. A. O's. There was a complete Bearer Service the whole evacuation from front to H.A.R.	

1875 Wt. W593/826 1,000,000 4/15 J.B.C. & A. A.D.S.S./Forms/C. 2118.

3 Volume XII Secret

WAR DIARY
or
INTELLIGENCE SUMMARY
(Erase heading not required.)

Army Form C. 2118

136 Field Ambulance
1/1st Division
Mob. at France 10p.m 5/1c

Place	Date 1917	Hour	Summary of Events and Information	Remarks and references to Appendices
FINS	May 6		On the night May 5/6th at 1.30 am I was favoured with the North Battalions and two large motor cars to FIFTEEN RAVINE and there looked up the cases which had come in. The total casualties whilst hard fighting the battalions was 186 Officers & 5 Sisters in O.R. being 185. With few exceptions there was all dressed by stretcher on May 6th. Preparation had been made for a much larger number of casualties. The worsts of the cases were not difficult to carry all being comparatively short. It was expected that a party would have to be out to ground for wounded on the night of May 1/2 but these were not arriving. Reports were sent in that So far as could be ascertained all wounded had been cleared. The instructions I had from the S/S. Brigade remained practically unaltered during the operation There was no change made in the location of the bearer post. Soup kitchens were established at the R.D.S. and at Queen Cross. The evacuation of wounded from FINS was nearly done, the C.R.D.S being within 800 yards (by RV18c) of the Field Amb. Bearing Post. The nursing, clerical and administration work at FINS was carried out by A Section. B & C sections are on duty at the Corps Rest Station YEBER. The Corps have is being re-opened to accept May 10/31st. 10th Div Rerve – see Appendix II Appendix III Evacuation Return May 1st —	Appendix I Enclosed Recpts May 10/11

JCRR

Army Form C. 2118

WAR DIARY
or
INTELLIGENCE SUMMARY
(Erase heading not required.)

Column XII Sect

136 Field Ambulance
40th Division
Army of France 20,000
57c

Instructions regarding War Diaries and Intelligence Summaries are contained in F.S. Regs., Part II. and the Staff Manual respectively. Title Pages will be prepared in manuscript.

Place	Date 1917	Hour	Summary of Events and Information	Remarks and references to Appendices
FINS	May 13		Capt. DOTTRIDGE, A.C. returned for duty, YPR	
"	May 15		Lt. ARMISTEAD detailed for temporary duty with 12th Suffolks, YPR	
"	May 16		Divisional bath opened at FINS following arrangements but made by the Conf. for XV Corps. Resuscitation	
"	May 18		1 Officer, 2 N.C.O. & 1 R. proceeded from BOIS de L'ABBÉ to take over HEBUTERNE. for Officer. No Officers and Patient is about 3 miles from HEBUTERNE. YPR	
"			Capt. MACKENZIE reported for temporary duty took this over YPR	
"	May 21		Capt. R. RUTHERFORD detailed for duty with 11th A.& S. Highlanders. YPR	
"	May 26		CAPT. T. BROOKE reported for duty	
"			Divisional Front changed upon 27 May 25 P.G. New evacuation scheme started. Appendix IV. There are no difficulties to report regarding new evacuation scheme except the inception that it was found a little difficult to keep communication with R.M.O's. Cases are carried YPR	
"	May 28		Lt. Qr. Mr. W. GOODLEY arrived for duty	
"			Instruction issued that the accommodation for wounded is to be increased at the two A.D.S. in tents a few yards from the bordure at the Boyer Infantry. YPR	
"	May 29		Capt. DOTTRIDGE detailed for duty with 11th A.& S. Highlanders	
"			CAPT. WESTLAKE reported for duty protection	
"			CAPT. MACKENZIE left unit on authorised 5 Spontaneous YPR	
"			CAPT. GAFFIKIN detailed for temporary duty at private burn	
"	May 31		CAPT. J.J. ARMISTEAD returned to the unit from 12th Suffolks.	
			On duty on return to unit he was made Mortuary & Latrine Corp. Officer.	

J.A. Ridsway Major
R.A.M.C.

App I

EVACUATION SCHEME OF FRONT LINE 40th DIVISION.
HEADQUARTERS, 136, FIELD AMBULANCE. R.A.M.C.

A. D. S. clearing the left of the Division is at Q 20 d 1.3. Distance from Headquarters, 4,800 yds. Very good road for Ambulance Cars.

PERSONNEL. 1 Officer and 19 other ranks. Two Horse Ambces. 1 Ford Car, and seven wheeled stretchers are at the disposal of the Officer in charge of the A.D.S. at Metz. Horse Ambulances and Motor Cars can proceed along the METZ- GOUZEACOURT Road to Q 26 c 5.0. Bearer Posts are situated as follows:-

1. Q 21 b Central. Personnell, 5 other ranks, distance from A.D.S. 1,000 yds. Evacuation by wheeled stretchers.

Left R. A. P. Q22 a 1.8, (in a Quarry). 6 other ranks, R.A.M.C. distance from No. 1 post, 500 yds., evacuation by wheeled stretchers.

Right Btn R.A.P. R 13 Central. Personnel, 8 other ranks, R.A.M.C. Distance from No. 4 Post - 900 yds. Evacuation by wheeled stretcher.

No. 4 Bearer Post is at Q 18 d 0.5. Personnel, 1 N.C.O., 5 other ranks, R.A.M.C. Evacuation to No. 3 bearer Post by hand carry. Distance 1,000 yds.

No. 3 Bear Post. Q 23 c 8.2. Personnel, 4 other ranks, Evacuation to No. 2 Bearer Post by wheeled stretcher, distance 1,300 yds.

No. 2 Bearer Post. Q 27 d 8.7. Personnel, 1 N.C.O., 4 other ranks. Evacuation to A.D.S. Metz - distance 1,300 yds, by wheeled stretcher or by Ambulance Cars.

A.D.S. clearing the Right of the Division, is situated at Q 29 D 2.9 in a sunken road. Personnel, 2 Officers, 20 other ranks. Two Horse Ambulances, one Ford Car, are at the disposal of the Officer in charge, and are accomodated at Queen's Cross. The route the Cars take from Fins is as follows:- FINS)GOUZEACOURT Road to the cross roads at W. 3 c 5.8. Then across country by track to Queen's Cross, Q 28 d 4.3, then 500 yds along METZ-GOUZEACOURT Road towards Gouzeacourt.

Continued, 2.

Thence by track to the A.D.S. Distance, 6,000 yds. If necessary, at night-time, cars can be sent further forward to Q 30 b 5.2. on the Trescault-Gouzeaucourt Road. 100 yds East along this road, by track again to R 19 c 9.3. on the Gouzeaucourt-Villiers-Plouich Road, along this road as far as 15 Ravine. Bearer Posts are situated as follows:-

1. 15 Ravine. R 19 b 1.1.
2. 16 Ravine. R 20 a 2.9.
3. R 21 b 5.2
4. R 20 d 6.4.
5. Quarry, R 26 d 3.9.
6. Q 30 b 5.4.

The number of bearers at these posts have varied from day to day. Nos. 1, 2, 3, 4 & 5 are combined with R.A.P. Evacuations as far as 15 Ravine can be done by car at night-time, and during the day by wheeled stretcher to the A.D.S. The distance of carriage by bearers in all these cases is not great.

10th May, 1917.

F. E. Rowand Robson
Lt. Col. R.A.M.C.
O/C. 136, Field Ambce.

Volume XII
Appendix F

SECRET. Appendix II Volume XII

Copy NO. 10.

40th Division R.A.M.C. Operation Order No. 26.

Reference Map 57 c 1/40.000.

The Corps front will be adjusted as follows:-

1. (a) Night 12/13th May.
120th Infantry Brigade will be relieved by the 60th Inf. Bde., 20th Division in its present area (less EQUANCOURT)

(b) The present Southern boundary of the 120th Infantry Bde. is R.Z.d.5.9. - Q.23.c.7.2. - Q22.d.O.C. - Q.27.c.3.5.

(c) Command to pass 10 a.m. 13th Instant.

(d) After relief, the 120th Infantry Bde. will become Brigade Reserve to the 8th Division in place of the 24th Brigade and will be accomodated as follows:-
    SOREL   Brigade Headquarters and 1 Battalion.
    HEUDECOURT 2 Battalions, T.M. Battery and M.G. Coy.
    DESSART WOOD. 1 Battalion.

(2) (a) Night 13th/14th May.
120th Infantry Bde. will relieve the 23rd Infantry Bde. in the left Bde. Sector of the 8th Divisional Front.

(b) Command to pass on completion of relief.

3. (a) Night 13th/14th May.
The 121st Infantry Bde will be relieved by the 60th Infantry Bde. 20th Division in its present area.

(b) Command to pass on completion of relief.

(c) The Southern Boundary up to which the 60th Infantry Bde. will take over will be R.14.d.0.1. - R.14.c.3.3. - R.19.b.4.0 - Q.32.d.6.0. - W.2.a.5.5. - W.2.a.4.2. - W.1.a.9.1. V.6.d.1.0 - along road through V.6. central - P.35. central to the present boundary P.35.a.7.3.
This will then be the boundary between the 29th and 40th Divisions.

(d) After relief, the 121st Infantry Brigade will become reserve Brigade to the 8th Division and will accomodated as in paragraph 1. (d) except that Brigade Headquarters may remain in DESSART WOOD.

4. The command of the whole front taken over by the 29th will pass to the G.O.C., 20th Division at 10 a.m. 14th May

5. (a) Night 14th/15th May.
The 121st Infantry Brigade will relieve the 25th Infantry Bde. in the Right Bde Sector of the 8th Division.

(b) Command to pass on completion of reliefs.

6. The command of the 8th Division Front will pass to the 40th Division at 10 a.m. 15th May.

7. 136th Field Ambulance will remain at FINS and be responsible for the evacuation of sick and wounded from the left and centre Brigades, taking over from the 24th Field Ambulance 8th Division, the Advanced Dressing Station in X 1.a.5.9. and Bearer Posts, clearing to that point ; by 6 p.m. 13th inst.

8. 137th Field Ambulance (less sufficient personnel to run a detention Hospital at MANANCOURT and the baths at ETRICOURT) will move from MANANCOURT to HEUDICOURT on the 14th inst. and will take over Dressing Station and Bearer Posts from 24th Field Ambulance 8th Division; and be responsible for the evacuation of sick and wounded from the Right Brigade.

9. Details of relief to be arranged between the O.C's concerned.

10. Divisional Headquarters will close at MANANCOUR at 10 a.m. 15th May and open at GURLU WOOD at the same hour.

11 Acknowledge.

Issued at 6 p.m.

(Signed A. J. Luther.
Col.
A.D.M.S. 40th Division.

11/5/17.

Appendix III Scheme III

EVACUATION SCHEME OF LEFT AND CENTRE BRIGADES, FRONT LINE.
40th DIVISION.

LEFT BRIGADE. (Map Ref. 1 in 20,000)
Sheet 57c S.E.

A.D.S. at Q 29 c. 9.9. (Sunken Road) Personnel - 1 Officer. 16 other ranks. Accomodation, 4 lying cases. Further accomodation is being prepared. A Horse Ambulance and a Ford Car are kept at the disposal of the Officer in charge of the A.D.S, and are kept North of Queen's Cross. Cases are evacuated via METZ to FINS, or across Country to QUEEN'S CROSS, and thence to FINS-GOUZEACOURT Road, meeting that road at W 3 C 5.7. - thence to FINS, a distance of 6,000 yds.

BEARER POSTS.

1. Quarry - R 25 D 2.9.

2. Re-lay Post - Q 30 B 5.3.

Regimental Aid Posts. One Battalion in the Line - (17th Welsh) are at Quarry Q 25 D 2.9. Battn. in support - (19th R.W.F) R.A.P. Q 30 D 8.8. Two Battalions in reserve - 18th Welsh & 12th S.W.B.) - in DESSART WOOD. Cases are carried on stretchers from the Quarry to the Re-lay Post by wheeled stretcher from the Re-lay Post to the A.D.S. - Distance from Quarry to Re-lay Post - 750 yds. - from Re-lay Post to A.D.S. - 900 yds.

CENTRE BRIGADE.

A.D.S. X A 2.9. (In a trench beside the Railway Line). Personnel - 1 N.C.O. - 8 other ranks. Accomodation - 6 lying cases. The accomodation is being increased.
Evacuation by stretchers by hand carriage, to a point - W 6 A 2.6 on the GOUZEACOURT- REVELON Road - distance 950 yds, - then by wheeled stretcher along the GOUZEACOURT-REVELON Road to W 11 C 6.5. - distance, 2,000 yds, where they are loaded on to a horse ambulance, then evacuated by HEUDECOURT to FINS. - distance 5,300 yds. At night-time, Ambulance Cars - horse and motor - can proceed to W 6 A 2.6. Alternative evacuation routs of evacuation. Hand Carriage from A.D.S. to Post Office, GOUZEAUCOURT - Q 36 D 4.9., then by horse or motor ambulance direct to FINS. Distance from A.D.S. to Post Office - 1,000 yds. - from Post Office to FINS, 6,500 yds.

COMBINED R.A.P. and BEARER POST.

Left Btn. (K.O.R.L.) R 26 C 5.0. (Sunken Road)
Right Btn.(H.L.I.) X2B 9.2. Four Bearers at each of these posts. The distances of each from A.D.S. is 1,500 yds. Evacuation from the Left Btn. by stretcher, hand carried, to A.D.S. From Right Btn,- by wheeled stretcher along the VILLIERS-GOUSLAIN ROUZEAUCOURT Road to R 31 D 5.2. - thence by hand carriage to A.D.S.
Support Btn. (A. & S. H.) R 31 D 2.4. - 400 yds from the A.D.S. Evacuation by hand carry.
Btn. in reserve (E. Surrey) R.A.P. W12 B 6.8. Four bearers to be attached. Evacuation by hand carriage to Ambulance Cars at W 11 C 6.5. - thence to FINS.

May 14th. 1917

F. E. Rowand Robinson
Lt. Col. R.A.M.C.
Comdg. 136 F.Amb.

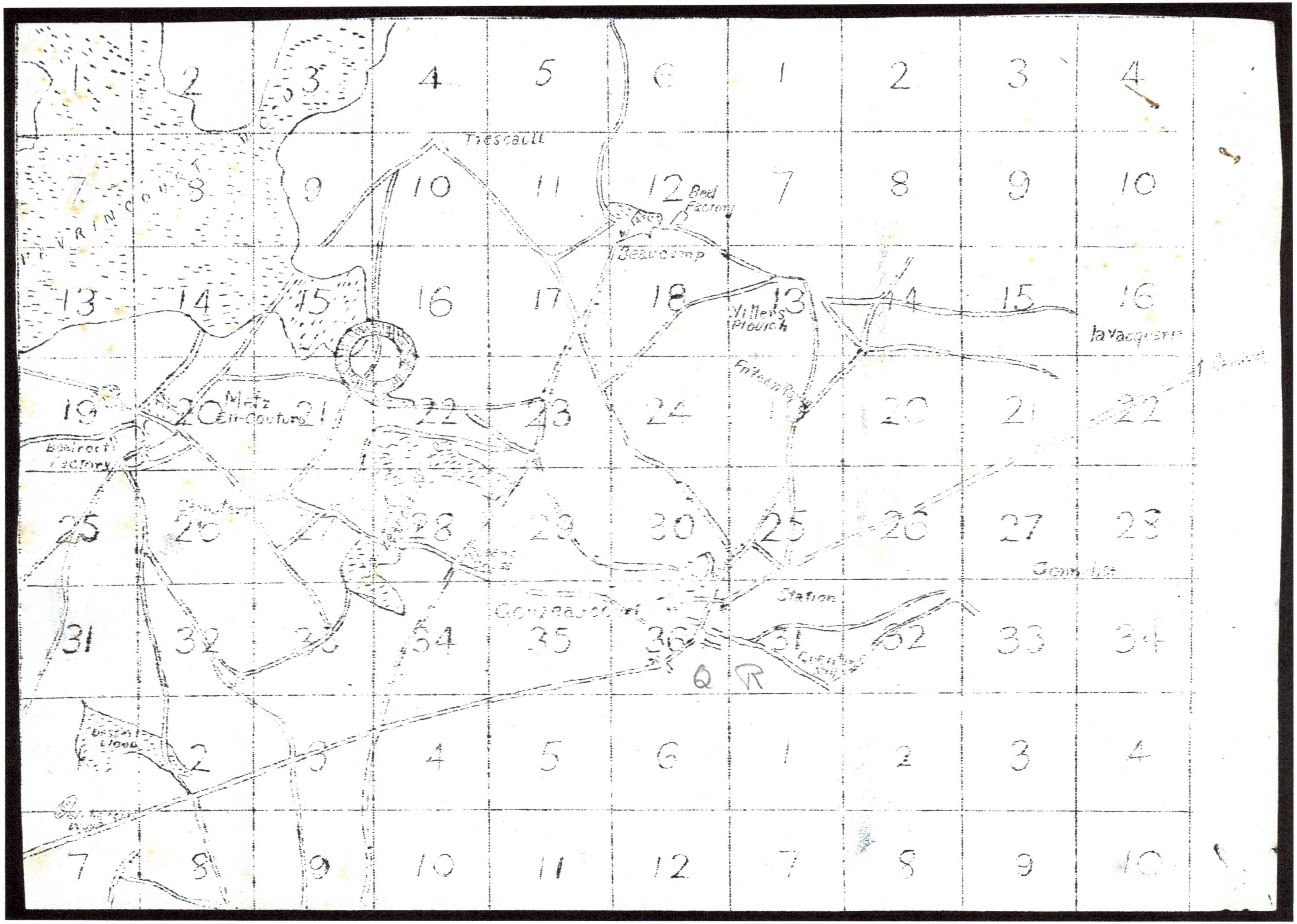
Trescault
Bed Factory
Beaucamp
Villers Plouch
la Vacquerie
Metz en Couture
Gonnelieu
Station
Gouzeaucourt
Dessart Wood
Q R

140/2230

No. 136th. F.A.

June 1917.

COMMITTEE FOR THE
MEDICAL HISTORY OF THE WAR
Date — 7 AUG. 1917

Army Form C. 2118
Secret

WAR DIARY
or
INTELLIGENCE SUMMARY
(Erase heading not required.)

136 Field Ambulance
40th Division
Map ref France 57c 40,000

Volume XIII

Place	Date Hour	Summary of Events and Information	Remarks and references to Appendices
FINS J.12.B	June 1st 1917	Arrangements for the evacuation of sick & wounded remain the same. Appendix No 1 in a copy of the scheme.	H.R.R.
"	" 2nd "	Capt. F. BROOKE detailed for duty at the left O.D.S.	
"	" 3rd "	Capt. F. BROOKE returned for duty with 24th Field Ambulance 8th Division.	
"	" 5th "	Capt. P.J. GAFFIKIN proceeds to D.R.S. Houtke Camp for duty.	
"	" 6th "	Capt. FOULKES Returned from temporary duty with 12th Suffolk Regt. YPRES
"	" 8th "	Lt. ARMISTEAD Returned from temporary duty with 12th Suffolk Regt. YPRES
"	" 9th "	Capt. FOULKES to Lt. O.D.S. for duty	
"	" "	Capt. BERRY & Lt. ARMISTEAD admitted to hospital YPRES	
"	" "	Capt. RIVERS POLLOCK reported for duty. Capt. BERRY and Lt. ARMISTEAD marched to the Base YPRES	
"	" "	Capt. E.A. MEADEN reported for duty.	
"	" "	It was decided that in order to relieve the personnel in the front line to join up the Repair A.D.S. and to evacuate cases from the Piper Brigade through the Quarry at P 95.a.0.9.	
"	" "	An arrangement was carried out gradually and completed by June 12th. YPRES	
"	" "	The evacuation scheme in the form of an Appendix (No 2) YPRES	
"	" 19th "	The new evacuation scheme for evacuation by the Decauville Railway Appendix (No 3) YPRES	
"	" "	Report on the arrangement for evacuation	
"	" 13th "	Capt. PALMER reported for duty.	
"	" "	Capt. FOULKES duties for temporary duty with 114th H.I. YPRES	
"	" "	Capt. MEADEN proceeded on leave	
"	" 15th "	Capt. RIVERS POLLOCK detailed for temporary duty with H.Q. Staff 17th Welsh. YPRES	
"	" "	Capt. DOTTRIDGE returned from duty with A.S.C.	
"	" 14th "	Capt. JARDINE Prcr H. RAMC. for temporary duty. Appendix (4) An amended evacuation scheme YPRES	
"	" 20th "	Capt. BEVERIDGE details for temporary duty with 18th Bart. Surreys YPRES	

1875 Wt. W593/826 1,000,000 4/15 J.B.C. & A. A.D.S.S./Forms/C. 2118.

Army Form C. 2118

WAR DIARY
or
INTELLIGENCE SUMMARY
(Erase heading not required.)

136 Field Ambulance
40th Div
Chief of France 57.40.000 Vol 13

Place	Date 1917	Hour	Summary of Events and Information	Remarks and references to Appendices
FINS	Jun 21st		Capt. O.C. DOTTRIDGE detailed for temporary duty with 20th Middlesex Regt.	
"	" 22		Capt. RIVERS POLLOCK returned from temporary duty with 17th Welsh Regt. #RR	
"	" 24		Lieut. H.R. SINCLAIR arrived for duty #RR	
"			Accommodation of the hospital is being increased. Two new huts are being erected. #RR	
"	" 28		Lieut. SINCLAIR detailed for duty with 17th Welsh Regt. #RR	
"	29		Capt. MEADON returned from leave. #RR	
"	30		Capt. FOULKES returned from temporary duty with 11th H.L.I. #RR. Since Jun 25th have been performing the duties of ?/?/ADMS ?/11th Division in addition to O.C. 136 F Amb.	

St Cormac Pattison
1st Lt Reserve
Comdt 136 F Amb

Appendix No 1

EVACUATION SCHEME OF FRONT LINE, 40th DIVISION.

Map Ref. FRANCE 57c.S.E. - 1/20,000.

Two Brigades in the Line.

Headquarters of Field Ambulance situated at V.12.b. FINS.

Evacuation from Left Brigade. A.D.S. situated at Q.29.b.2.9. Personnel - 2 Officers, 16 other ranks. Two horse ambulances and one Ford Car are at the disposal of the Officer in charge. The cars are accomodated North of Queen's Cross. Accomodation for 12 lying cases. (Arrangements have been made to extend this accomodation). The route the cars take from FINS is as follows:-
To QUEEN'S CROSS via METZ, then to Q.29.c.0.0. on the METZ-GOUZEAUCOURT Road, then by track to the A.D.S. - distance, 8,200 yds. Road good, except at QUEEN'S CROSS, which is being repaired. At night-time, cars can proceed as far as No. 15 Ravine, - distance, 3,000 yds.

Bearer Posts are situated as follows:-
1. Q.30.d.8.8. 6 Bearers. Accomodation for 2 lying cases. Distance from A.D.S. - 900 yds. Evacuation by wheeled stretcher during the day, and by car at night.
2. R.25.d.2.9. 8 Bearers. Evacuation by wheeled stretcher to No. 1 Bearer Post. Distance 1,200 yds. It is proposed to make a Battle Aid Post at this Quarry, to accomodate 40 patients.

R.A.P. Left Battalion. R.19.a.5.4. Distance from No. 1 Bearer Post, 1,500 yds. Evacuation by wheeled stretcher by day, and by car at night. Four bearers are stationed at this R.A.P.

R.A.P. Right Battalion. R.20.a.2.9. Evacuation by wheeled stretcher to No. 1 Bearer Post. Distance, 2,000 yds. Four bearers are stationed at this R.A.P.

R.A.P. of Battalion in reserve,- DESSART WOOD.

R.A.P. of Battalion in Support,- Q.30.d.8.7. Distance from No. 1 Bearer Post - 100 yds. Owing to the close proximity of this R.A.P. to No. 1 Bearer Post, no R.A.M.C. Bearers are attached.

Evacuation from the Left Brigade.

A.D.S. X.a.2.9. (In a trench beside the Railway Line) Personnel - 1 N.C.O. - 8 other ranks. Accomodation, 6 lying cases. The accomodation is being increased. Evacuation by stretchers by hand carriage to a point - W.6.a.2.6. on the GOUZEAUCOURT-REVELON Road - distance 950 yds.,- then by wheeled stretcher along the GOUZEAUCOURT-REVELON Road to W.11.c.6.5. - distance, 2,000 yds., where they are loaded on to a horse ambulance, then evacuated by HEUDECOURT to FINS - distance, 5,500 yds. At night-time, ambulance cars - horse and motor - can proceed to W.6.a.2.6 Alternative evacuation route - Hand carriage from A.D.S. to Post Office, GOUZEAUCOURT - Q.36.d.4.9. then by horse or motor ambulance direct to FINS. Distance from A.D.S. to Post Office - 1,000 yds. - from Post Office to FINS, 6,500 yds. Four bearers are stationed at the Post Office.

R.A.P. Battalion in the Line. R.31.b.8.9. 4 R.A.M.C. bearers attached to this Post.

R.A.P. Battalion in Support. R.31.c.9.5. (In a Quarry).

Battalion in Reserve. R.A.P. W.6.d.central.
Evacuation from R.A.P. of Btn. in the Line is by wheeled stretcher - hand carry - distance, 1,500 yds. to A.D.S.
Evacuation from Support Btn. by hand carriage to A.D.S. - distance, 500 yds.
Evacuation from the Btn. in Reserve, by wheeled stretcher to the horse ambulance at W.6.a.2.6.

June 1st 1917

Appendix No 2

EVACUATION SCHEME OF FRONT LINE, 40th DIVISION.

Map Ref. FRANCE 57 c. S.E. - 1/20,000.

Two Brigades in the Line.

Headquarters of Field Ambulance situated at V.12.b. FINS.

Evacuation from the Left Brigade.

A.D.S. situated at Q.29.d.2.9. Personnel 1 Officer, 16th other ranks. One horse ambulance and one Ford Car are at the disposal of the Officer in charge. The Cars are accomodated North of Queen's Cross. Accomodation - 14 lying cases, and 14 sitting cases. Further accomodation for 14 lying cases will shortly be ready. Cases are evacuated from the A.D.S. in Cars or wheeled stretchers to the Loading Point at Q.27.d.8.8. Here they are placed on a Decaville Truck - by rail to FINS. Distance from the A.D.S. to Loading Point - 1,500 yds. At FINS the truck is unloaded, and the patients hand-carried to the Dressing Station, - distance, 200 yds.

Bearer Posts are situated as follows;-
1. Q.30.d.8.8. 6 Bearers. Accomodation for 2 lying cases. Distance from A.D.S. - 900 yds. Evacuation by wheeled stretcher during the day, and by car at night.

2. R.25.d.2.9. 11 Bearers. Evacuation by wheeled stretcher to No. 1 Bearer Post. Distance 1,200 yds. A Battle Aid Post is being made at this Quarry, to accomodate 40 patients.

R.A.P. Left Battalion. R.19.a.5.4. Distance from No. 1 Bearer Post, 1,500 yds. Evacuation by wheeled stretcher by day, and by car at night. Four bearers are stationed at this R.A.P.

R.A.P. Right Battalion. R.20.a.2.9. Evacuation by wheeled stretcher to No. 1 Bearer Post. Distance, 2,000 yds. Four Bearers are stationed at this R.A.P.

R.A.P. of Battalion in Reserve - DESSART WOOD.

R.A.P. of Battalion in Support - Q.30.d.8.7. Distance from No. 1 Bearer Post - 100 yds. Owing to the close proximity of this R.A.P. to No. 1 Bearer Post, no R.A.M.C. Bearers are attached.

Evacuation from the Right Brigade.

A.D.S. X.1.a.2.9. (In a trench beside the Railway Line) Personnel - 1 N.C.O. - 8 other ranks. Accomodation, 9 lying cases and 20 sitting. Evacuation from the A.D.S. to the loading point of the Decauville Railway at Q.35.d.3. Here, cases are loaded on to a truck by rail to FINS.

R.A.P. of Battalion in the Line - R.26.d.7.7. ~~4 R.A.M.C. bearers attached to this Post.~~

R.A.P. of Battalion in Support - R.31c.9.5.

R.A.P. of Battalion in Reserve - W.3.d.9.5.

EVACUATION SCHEME, Contd.

Bearer Post, R.31.b.8.9.   1 N.C.O. and 4 Bearers.

Cases are evacuated from the Battalion in the Line to this Bearer Post. Distance 1,000 yds. Hand carried. From the Bearer Post to the A.D.S. by hand carry, - distance, 1,250 yds. Cases from the Battalion in Support, by hand carriage to A.D.S. - distance, 500 yds.   A Motor Car is sent to the Reserve R.A.P. when required.

12/6/17.

[signature]

Lieut-Col., R.A.M.C.

O/C. 136th Field Ambulance.

Appendix No 3

To:- A. D. M. S.,
      40th Division.

Sick and Wounded were evacuated from the Right and Left A.D.S's. by the Decauville Railway yesterday evening. One petrol engine and one truck to each A.D.S.

The Truck is fitted with a framework, to carry eight lying cases, and six sitting.

The trucks are easily loaded, and it takes only about five minutes to complete a load.

The Train from left A.D.S. took 30 minutes - that from Right A.D.S. 40 minutes, to reach FINS.

The present arrangement is that the Railway Operating Company will send a truck up when it is required. This will be quite satisfactory when the telephone is ready. It is not yet complete.

The loading point for Right A.D.S. is at Q.35.d.6.3. Here accomodation for patients awaiting removal, already exists. Two Bearers will remain at the Loading Point to assist in loading, and to send telephone messages.

The loading point of Left A.D.S. is at Q.27.b.8.8. Here it is proposed to build a shelter for patients awaiting removal. Two Bearers will also be kept here.

The unloading point at FINS is situated at V.12.c.7.8. Distance to Field Ambulance - 200 yds.

12/6/17.

Capt. R.A.M.C.
for O/C. 136th Field Ambce.

Appendix (4)

EVACUATION SCHEME OF FRONT LINE, 40th DIVISION.

Map Ref. FRANCE 57.c.S.E. - 1/20,000.

Two Brigades in the Line.

Headquarters of Field Ambulance situated at V.12.b. FINS.

Evacuation from the Left Brigade.

A.D.S. for Left and Right Brigades situated at Q.29.d.2.9. Personnel, 1 Officer, 16 other ranks. One Horse Ambulance and One Ford Car are at the disposal of the Officer in Charge. The cars are accomodated North of QUEEN'S CROSS. Accomodation, 14 lying cases, and 14 sitting cases. Further accomodation for 14 lying cases will shortly be ready. Cases are evacuated from the A.D.S. in Cars or wheeled stretchers to the Leading Point at Q.27.d.5.8. Here they are placed on a Decauville Truck - by rail to FINS. Distance from the A.D.S. to Leading Point, 1,500 yds. At FINS the Truck is unloaded, and the patients hand-carried to the Dressing Station - distance, 200 yds. During normal times, one Truck calls daily at the Leading Point at 5-30 p.m. During active operations, six trucks will be available.

Bearer Posts are situated as follows:-
1. Q.30.d.8.8. 6 Bearers. Accomodation for 2 lying cases. Distance from A.D.S. 900 yds. Evacuation by wheeled stretcher during the day, and by Car at night.

R.A.P. Left Battalion. R.19.a.5.4. Distance from No. 1 Bearer Post, 1,500 yds. Evacuation by wheeled stretcher by day, and by car at night. Four bearers are stationed at this R.A.P.

R.A.P. Right Battalion. R.20.a.2.9. Evacuation by wheeled stretcher to No. 1 Bearer Post - Distance, 2,000 yds. 4 Bearers are stationed at this R.A.P.

R.A.P. of Battalion in Reserve - Q.29.b.2.1. Owing to the close proximity of this R.A.P. to A.D.S. no R.A.M.C. Bearers are attached.

R.A.P. of Battalion in Support - Q.30.b.1.8. Evacuation by wheeled stretcher to No. 1 Bearer Post - 500 yds.

Evacuation from the Right Brigade.

Bearer Posts are situated as follows:-
1. R.31.b.8.9. Personnel, 1 N.C.O. and 4 other ranks. Accomodation, 2 lying cases. Evacuation to No. 2 Bearer Post - distance, 500 yds.
2. R.25.d.2.9. Personnel, 11 Bearers. Accomodation for 48 patients will be available in a few days time. Evacuation by wheeled stretcher to Bearer Post at Q.30.d.8.8. thence to A.D.S. situated at Q.29.d.2.9. (Vide evacuation of Left Brigade, above).

R.A.P. of Right Battalion in the Line - R.26.d.7.7.
R.A.P. of Left Battalion in the Line - R.25.d.2.9.
R.A.P. of Battalion in Support - R.31.c.9.5.
R.A.P. of Battalion in Reserve - W.3.d.9.5.

Cases are evacuated from the Right Battalion in the Line to the Bearer Post at R.31.b.8.9. - distance, 1,000 yds. hand carried.※
Cases are evacuated from the Left Battalion in the Line through Bearer Post at R.25.d.2.9. (as above)
Cases from the Battalion in Support by hand carriage to No. 2 Bearer Post (Quarry) - distance, 1,500 yds.
A Motor Car is sent to the Reserve R.A.P. when required.

※ and thence to the Quarry at R.25.d.2.9.

F.E. Rowand Robinson
Lieut-Col. R.A.M.C.
O/C. 136th Field Ambulance.

June 17th 1917

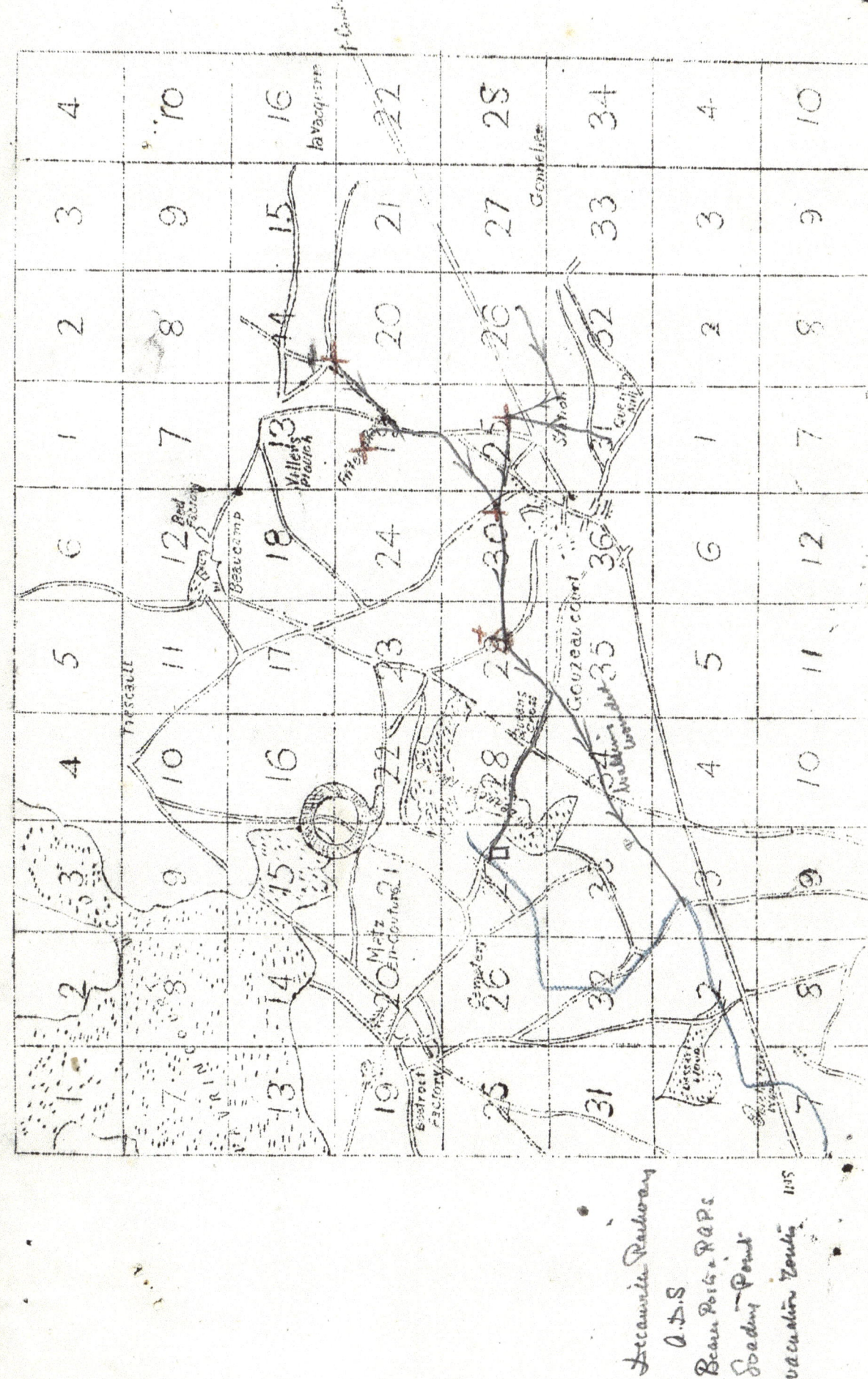

COMMITTEE FOR THE
MEDICAL HISTORY OF THE WAR
Date 10 SEP. 1917

No. 136. 7 a.

WAR DIARY or INTELLIGENCE SUMMARY

Army Form C. 2118

Volume XIV Secret

136 Field Ambulance 40th Division
Map of France 57c   1:40,000

Place	Date	Hour	Summary of Events and Information	Remarks and references to Appendices
FINS	1917			
	1.7.17		Capt. FOULKES returned from duty with 14 H.L.I. and reported for duty.	
	6.7.17		Capt. MEADEN proceeded on temporary M.D. to 11 K.O.R.L. H.Q.R. followed battn. into the line	
	7.7.17		Capt. CAFFIKIN admitted from Headquarter Fourth Army than YRA	
	8.7.17		6 O.R. Reinforcements arrived	
	9.7.17		Capt. RIVERS POLLOCK proceeded to 115 K.O.R.L. in relief of Capt. MEADEN	
	10.7.17		Capt. MEADEN returned to permanent duty with 20th Division H.Q.R. The unit took over from the Corps Horse Breaking Station in order to horses an to 40th Division Horse Depot Station. The relief was completed by 3rd day. 135 Field Ambulance took over the head quarters of this unit at Fins. Capt. DOTTRIDGE returned from the 20th Middlesex YRA 135 Field Ambulance bearers and parties of the personnel of this unit went at the O.D.S. and its personnel attached to the R.A.P.'s YRA	
	11.7.17		16 men leave tents to-day YRA.	
	12.7.17		Relief completed to-day. He remained at the A.D.S. until the time being from	
	13.7.17		Capt. MOHAN returned to headquarter with them men arr. YRA	
	14.7.17		from Quite familiar with their work YRA	
	15.7.17		Lt SINCLAIR returned from 14th Welsh. YRA	
			Proceeded to LIERAMONT (62c E 13o) to make out a site for a A.R.D.S. the site picked a Captain of instruction to form a Corps Horse Breaking Station. A plan of them area in from Army Hd to with a copy of which was by attached	
	16.7.17		Capt MOHAN proceeded to 19th W.Y. for temporary duty. YRA.	
	17.7.17		Handed over the Corps H.D.C. 136 F.Amb. to Capt. P.E. CAFFIKIN R.A.M.C.S.R. and then proceeded on leave. Joint war station. LLOYDBANK	

Vol XIV page 2

WAR DIARY
or
INTELLIGENCE SUMMARY

Army Form C. 2118

136 Field Ambulance 49 Div.
SECRET   MAP REF FRANCE 1/40000 57C

Place	Date	Hour	Summary of Events and Information	Remarks and references to Appendices
FINS	18-7-17	12 noon	Reassigned in command of unit from Lt Col S.E. ROWAN-ROBINSON to be Second Capt of 136	
	23-7-17		Capt D.H. PALMER proceeded to 405 Div Engineers for temporary duty	
			Capt R. HEWITT returned from duty at II Corps Reinforcement Camp and was	
	29/7/17		Capt A. MYERS TOLLEY returned from ordinary leave 7" to 17" K.O.R.L. days 8	
	25/7/17		Capt G.A. DOTTERIDGE T 24 O.R. left for returning sick 34 O.R.'s	
	27/7/17		108 reinforcement received from J.I.P.A. 64	
			Capt H. RUSH - RUSSELL returned to 49 Div. for duty	
	30/7/17		Lt.Col S.E. ROWAN ROBINSON returned from leave	
			Your in command of the Unit today on Westmoreland leave	

E. Pownam Robinson
Lt Col RAMC

14q/2304

No. 136. F.a.

Aug 1917

COMMITTEE FOR THE
MEDICAL HISTORY OF THE WAR
Date -1 OCT 1917

Army Form C. 2118

WAR DIARY
or
INTELLIGENCE SUMMARY
(Erase heading not required.)

136 Field Ambulance
40th Division
Map of France 57c

Place	Date 1917	Hour	Summary of Events and Information	Remarks and references to Appendices
FINS V.18d	1.8.17		The unit is still in charge of the Divisional Main Dressing Station	
	3.8.17		Besides the routine work the unit is occupied in making roads around the camp and erecting huts for the men. YPR	
	4.8.17		Lt. SINCLAIR (attached to 7th Guards) Entraining Bn today & is [?] of the Brigade's [?] YPR	
	6.8.17		Capt PALMER returned from detached duty with 10th Div R.E. YPR. Sports were held by the unit	
	7.8.17		Capt MOHAN returned from detached duty with 19 RWF	
			Lieut SCOTT returned to the unit (19 RWF) YPR	
	8.8.17		Capt P.J. GAFFIKIN proceeded on Quiet leave YPR	
	9.8.17		Capt HEWITT proceeded on leave YPR	
	10.9.17		Capt PROCTER reported from 135 Field Ambulance for temporary duty with this unit YPR	
			Capt GIBSON departs for duty with this unit YPR	
	15.8.17		Lt Dr GODLEY proceed on leave YPR	
	16.8.17		Capt PROCTER returned to 135 Field Ambulance	
	21.8.17		Received instructions to hand over D.A.D.S. to 137 Field Ambulance and to proceed to MOISLAINS to take over M Corps Rest Station One Section proceed today YPR	

Army Form C. 2118

Vol XV

136 Field Ambulance
40 Division

Map ref 62 c 1.40000

WAR DIARY
or
INTELLIGENCE SUMMARY
(Erase heading not required.)

Place	Date 1917	Hour	Summary of Events and Information	Remarks and references to Appendices
MOISLAINS C.18a	22.8.17		The Moor & Corps Rest Station were inspected by Colonel Mackay. Capt GIBSON proceeded to No 5 C.C.S for temporary duty	
	23.8.17		Capt DOTTRIDGE is Motois off the Strength from No 13 C.C.S for permanent duty	
	26.8.17		Capt McAFFEE, Capt LLOYD with one section of 105 H Amb arrived for duty. year Capt LLOYD to No 5 C.C.S for temporary duty Capt PALMER " " " " year Capt HEWITT returned from leave year	
	29.8.17		S/Sgt GOODLEY returned from leave year	
	30.8.17		Capt P.S CAFFIKIN attached to No 5 C.C.S Lt HUDDLESTON reported in duty	
	30.8.17		Capt PALMER returned from	

S/M Lieut Col Stephenson
1st Palmer
Com/1/136 F Amb.

Sept. 1917

No. 136. ? a.

14.04.08

COMMITTEE FOR THE
MEDICAL HISTORY OF THE WAR
Date -5 NOV.1917

WAR DIARY or INTELLIGENCE SUMMARY

Army Form C. 2118

Volume XVI a   Secret   136 Field Ambulance

Place	Date 1917	Hour	Summary of Events and Information	Remarks and references to Appendices
MOISLAINS C.18	1.9.17		The unit is employed in forming a/c to the III Corps Rest Station. The Festage accomm. station is being replaced by huts, Adrian, and Hospital Marquees.	
	3.9.17		Capt PALMER returned from 5.C.C.S. Capt J. Loyd (1057 A) returned from 5.C.C.S. Capt GAFFIKIN transferred to 135 F.Amb. Capt HUDDLESTON Reinforcement. Capt ROBERTSON return to the Strength of the unit but doing duty with 137 F.Amb. Lieut FAIRIE return to the Strength doing duty with A.D.M.S. 29 Division. A board of Officers proceeded to MANANCOURT for the purpose of ascertaining cause of the death of No. 7 Q.O. 6 Labour Company. Y.P.R.R. Capt HEWITT detailed for temporary duty with 17 F.Amb.	
	5.9.17		Capt MOHAN proceeded on six weeks leave and is struck off the strength. Y.P.R.R.	
	7.9.17		Capt LLOYD returned to 105 Field Amb. Capt HEWITT returns from 17 F.Amb. Y.P.R.R. A number of recommendations for good work in the field from the Depot of an above unit.	not attached
	9.9.17		Capt PALMER adjunct on leave Y.P.R.R.	
	3.6.9.M		Capt MCAFIE 10 O.R & 1,105 F.Amb reform their unit. Capt H.D.S. RICHARDS & 9 O.R of 2/1 West Lancashire Field Ambulance adjourn the Rest Station for duty. During construction took her has contact during the Adjust month. 5 admissions 3 austin huts Y.P.R.R. Station accommun. of up for 80 hours. True admissions testive infects to 1 for falling water. An incinerator for tenning fever & Rathein. 3 laufts	

1875. Wt. W593/826 1,000,000 4/15 J.B.C. & A. A.D.S.S./Forms/C. 2118.

Confidential.

Medical Services

War Diaries of

A.D.M.S. 40th Division.
O.C. 135th Field Ambulance.
O.C. 136th " "
O.C. 137th " "

For month of

October, 1917.

Vols. XVII.

H. Rowand Robinson
Lt. Col. RAMC
A/A.D.M.S. 40th Div.

Cor 1917

136 2nd Ault
9/07
17

140/2499.

COMMITTEE FOR THE
MEDICAL HISTORY OF THE WAR

Date -8 DEC. 1917

Army Form C. 2118

Secret

WAR DIARY
or
INTELLIGENCE SUMMARY
(Erase heading not required.)

136 Field Ambulance

Volume XVII

Instructions regarding War Diaries and Intelligence Summaries are contained in F.S. Regs., Part II. and the Staff Manual respectively. Title Pages will be prepared in manuscript.

Place	Date 1917	Hour	Summary of Events and Information	Remarks and references to Appendices
MOISLAINS	Oct 1		Capt. W.M. ROBERTSON Shown S/f Shrapnel injury	
C.12d.05	" 2		Capt. J.C. HILL Namely reported ordnance for duty. H.R.R.	
	" 7		3 A. O.R's returned from 20 C.C.S. H.R.R	
	" 8		Unit moved from Tin Cabs Rest Station MOISLAINS to PERONNE (FLAMICOURT) Ref.	
	" 10		A.S.C. attached Moved via BAPAUME to GUDY-EN-ARTOIS	
			R.A.M.C. entrained for GUDY-EN-ARTOIS arriving same day. H.R.R.	
			Baths at GUDY letters over and above at Same. H.R.R.	
	" 11		A.S.C. attached arrived at GUDY-EN-ARTOIS	
	" 12		Capt. GIBSON & J.O.R's returned from temporary duty at 20.5 C.C.S. H.R.R	
			Capt. PALMER Proc. and reported to 1.56 C.C.S for duty, in Radiographist Yearle S/ Shrapnel wounds	
	" 13		Horse transport inspected by D.C. Brit Dvis	
	" 16		Medical Records for Examination of Personnel 41st Div't from A.S.C. H.R.	
			Capt. WARD SMITH reported reports for duty with 135 F.Amb.	
	" 21		Capt. GATTIRIN arrived for duty	
			Took over the duties of A/ADMS to day Col ASHWORTH having departed on six days leave. H.R.R	
	" 29		The Unit moved from GUDY-EN-ARTOIS to LOCHEUX	
	" 31		Capt. GIBSON departed for permanent duty with 26 G.C.S.	

Howard Rattray
Lt Col R.A.M.C.

No. 136. 7. a.

COMMITTEE FOR THE
MEDICAL HISTORY OF THE WAR
Date 17 JAN. 1918

Army Form C. 2118

WAR DIARY
or
INTELLIGENCE SUMMARY
(Erase heading not required.)

Volume XVIII   of 1/30 Field Ambulance
                10th Division
                (Week ending
                    Nov. Rt. 57c ??)

Place	Date	Hour	Summary of Events and Information	Remarks and references to Appendices
LUCHEUX T/16	Nov 11		Capt. GIBSON went to No 9 C.C.S. for duty. A/S Steriffe + J.R.D.R. Court of Inquiry assembled at Unit Headquarters to enquire into an accident which occurred on the line of march.	
	Nov 13		Capt. P.S. GAFFIKIN, CAPT T.C. HEWITT joined Unit from leave. H.Q.R.	
	Nov 15		Capt. HILL posted to 148 Brigade R.T.O. for temporary duty. H.Q.R.	
	Nov 16		Capt. GAFFIKIN, Capt. HEWITT returned from leave. H.Q.R.	
COUYEU-ATTOIS P/02 & 5	Nov 17		Unit moved from LUCHEUX to COUY-EN-ARTOIS. H.Q.R.	
	Nov 18		Capt. HEWITT detailed for temporary duty at 91 C.C.S. H.Q.R.	Appendix I (Capt P.S.GAFFIKIN took over as O.C.)
COMIECOURT A 23 doc	Nov 19		Unit moved from GOUY-EN-ARTOIS to COMIECOURT H.Q.R.	Appendix II W.O.R.
BARASTRE 0.15 6.8.6	Nov 20		Unit moved from COMIECOURT to BARASTRE H.Q.R. 91. O.R. (Grown) proceeded to 137 Field Ambut. for duty H.Q.R.	Appendix III
	Nov 21		Capt. WARD SMITH P.A.M.C. reported for temporary duty H.Q.R.	
TRESCAULT Q.26	Nov 24		Unit moved from BARASTRE to TRESCAULT (57c. Q.2.6) Capt. WARD SMITH with 31 traces departed for duty with 137 F. Amb. H.Q.R.	Appendix IV (Capt P.S.GAFFIKIN took over as O.C.)
	Nov 26		Capt. HUDDLESTON, Capt. P.S. GAFFIKIN, Capt. WARD SMITH + 84 O.R. returned to H.Q. from 137 Field Ambulance. H.Q.R.	Appendix V
LECHELLES	Nov 27		Capt. AUDDLESTON (Capt. WARD SMITH + 84 O.R. returned to LECHELLES (57c. P.3.6)	W.O.R.
			Unit moved from TRESCAULT to LECHELLES au bois (57d E.5.2 centre)	Appendix VI
			Unit moved from LECHELLES to BIENVILLERS H.Q.R.	at BIENVILLERS
	Nov 29		Capt. GAFFIKIN + 39 O.R. referred for link. march from LECHELLES to BIENVILLERS	
			The remainder of the Unit marched from LECHELLES to 137 F. Amb. H.Q.R.	
	Nov 30		Capt. WARD SMITH returned to 131 F. Amb.	Appendix VII
			A/S Lotus MORE + L.BERNEY M.O.R.C. reported for duty on being posted to the Unit + A/S yen BERNEY W. to A/S.C.S.ACHIET-LE-GRAND today and to strength of Unit + return struck H.Q.R.	

J.W. Boissonnault ? Lt.
Comdt. 1/30 F.A.E.

1875 Wt. W593/826 1,000,000 4/15 J.B.C. & A.   A.D.S.S./Forms/C. 2118.

SECRET.

MAP REF 1/40,000 57c

Army Form C. 2118

Instructions regarding War Diaries and Intelligence Summaries are contained in F.S. Regs., Part II. and the Staff Manual respectively. Title Pages will be prepared in manuscript.

WAR DIARY
or
INTELLIGENCE SUMMARY

(Erase heading not required.)

136 FIELD AMBULANCE 40 DIV. VOLUME 18 APPENDIX 1 Page 1.

Place	Date	Hour	Summary of Events and Information	Remarks and references to Appendices
			On the morning of 25-11-17, I received orders to proceed from HAVRINCOURT to GRAINCOURT, & report to O.C. 137 F.A. at A.D.S. GRAINCOURT, taking with me volunteers from A.D.M.S. to O.C. 137 F.A. On arrival at A.D.S., I was instructed that I was to take a party of bearers & 9° personnel to search the area BOURLON WOOD, & BOURLON, for wounded. I added to as many bearers as possible from 136 F.A., & there were given me, reinforced by bearers of 135 & 137 F.A's. We then proceeded along the road GRAINCOURT – ANNEUX, but found the road wrecked along being heavily shelled. & therefore took the & ANNEUX village went the direction of ANNEUX CHAPEL. We sent party across country on the outskirts of ANNEUX CHAPEL, in the continuous heavy shell fire, chiefly 5.9" & 4.2" shells, in the areas E14, & T.E.30 & T6. Ultimately the party reached ANNEUX CHAPEL without casualty. Here I found the R.A.P's of 18 WELSH Regt. & 13 W.B. I established a relay bearer post here, & left for the front party with the wounded, & proceeded by the road ANNEUX	

SECRET   month of / appendix 57 & Army Form C. 2118

WAR DIARY
or
INTELLIGENCE SUMMARY
(Erase heading not required.) VULIE APPENDIX 1 Page 2

136 FIELD AMBULANCE, 40 DIV.

Place	Date	Hour	Summary of Events and Information	Remarks and references to Appendices

CHAPEL – BOURLON. The worst was also heavily shelled. On opening F.19 c. 3.9. I found R.A.P.s of 17th Welch, 13th A.&S.H., which I arranged to clear from the artillery barrage post. On reaching BOURLON WOOD, we proceeded to search it, & wounded found were to E.12 d. 6.6 in BOURLON village, where I found R.A.P.s 14 H.L.I. & 13 E. SURREY REGT. I cleared those parts & learnt that there were still wounded lying out in the village. Stories were found unfavourable to collect there, owing to enemy machine gun fire. An attempt was to be made at dawn next day, to get through the villages to relieve some companies which had been cut off, & I cleared to remove in later of gettingt the wounded in, but the attack did not come off. I notified situation to general situation to O.C. 137 F.A., who informed me that his unit was being relieved & that when relieved I was to return to TRESCAULT. Accordingly when about 6.30 p.m. I received a message from the O/C between 62 DIV, that he was establishing a post at F13 & 14, I could now take over the evacuation

SECRET.

WAR DIARY *or* **INTELLIGENCE SUMMARY**　Army Form C. 2118

(Erase heading not required.) VOLUME 18 APPENDIX 1 page 3

136 FIELD AMBULANCE, 40 DIV

of wounded, ? with some of troops 57 c.

of wounded, ? with down the Germans by the same route, as one had advanced by, again encountering heavy shelling & machine gun fire, ultimately around ANNEUX CHAPEL, but were fortunate to escape with but two men slightly wounded, and ? then brought to the front back to TRESCAULT & rejoined 136 FA next day.

R. J. Nesbit Griffiths
Captain RAMC
30/11/17

SECRET.

Army Form C.2118

WAR DIARY
or
INTELLIGENCE SUMMARY

Ref. map 57c / 40000   (Erase heading not required.)

136 Field Ambulance   VOLUME 18   APPENDIX II

Summary of Events and Information

The following casualties took place in the personnel of this Unit during the action of the 40th Division in BOURLON WOOD and the village of BOURLON on Nov 25th – 26th 1917.

E 12 central sheet 57c

No 69375	Pte	Brear O.L.	– Killed
No 69518	"	Elmer W.	– Killed
No 69545	"	Bennetto J.	– Died of wounds
No 69559	"	Brink J.	– Wounded
No 69476	"	Warburton J.	– Wounded
No 69602	"	Woods J.	– Wounded
No 69423	"	Taft J.	– Wounded
No 69861	"	Frith G.	– Wounded
No 90011	"	Batchelor J.	– Wounded
No 88995	"	Wilson R.	– Wounded
No 69475	"	Brown J.	– N.Y.D.N. (Sick)
No 69329	"	Osborn A.B.	– Wounded

Lt-Col. R.a.M.C.
O.C. 136 F. Ambce

Appendix III sheet I

Army Form W. 3121.

Brigade. 40th Div. Division. R.A.M.C. Corps. Date of Recommendation. 28/11/17.

Schedule No. (to be left blank)	Unit	Regtl. No.	Rank and Name	Action for which commended	Recommended by	Honour or Reward	(To be left blank)
	136th Field Ambulance	69588	STAFF SERGT. CHARLES HARRY PARKES.	This N.C.O. showed great courage, and was of the utmost assistance to me in taking the Bearers forward, and bringing them back again through heavy fire from enemy artillery and machine guns.	Lt.-Col. L. G. Rowan Robinson. Captain P. Jacob Gaskikin, R.A.M.C.	Military Medal.	
		69612	PTE. GEORGE SUTTON.	Showed great courage in collecting wounded under heavy fire.	do.	do.	
		51292	SERGT. WILLIAM Christopher ATKINSON LAING.	This N.C.O. was of great assistance to me in taking the Bearers forward and bringing them back again through heavy shelling and machine gun fire. He set a fine example of courage and coolness.	do.	do.	
		60665	PTE. ARTHUR WELLBORNE HAZELDINE.	Showed great courage in collecting wounded under heavy fire. The above occurred during the actions of the 40th Division in BOURLON WOOD, Map Ref. E.13. Sheet 57c.	do.	do.	

Appendix III. Sheet II. Army Form W. 3121.

Date of Recommendation. 29-11-17

Brigade. _____ Division. 40th _____ Corps. R.A.M.C.

Schedule No. (to be left blank)	Unit	Regtl. No.	Rank and Name	Action for which commended	Recommended by	Honour or Reward	(To be left blank)
3	136th Field Ambulance.	69320.	PTE. JOSEPH KEHOE	During the actions of that 40th Division in BOURLON WOOD, Map Ref. E.18., Sheet 57c. This man showed great courage and resource in collecting wounded under heavy fire, taking his squad right up to the Line.	Captain P. Jacob Geffkin R.A.M.C. [signature]	D.C.M.	

No. 136 T.A.

COMMITTEE FOR THE
MEDICAL HISTORY OF THE W..
Date -1 FEB. 1918

Army Form C. 2118

Secret Volume XIX
Page 1

WAR DIARY / 136 Field Ambulance
or
INTELLIGENCE SUMMARY
(Erase heading not required.)

Place	Date 1917	Hour	Summary of Events and Information	Remarks and references to Appendices
BIENVILLERS AU-BOIS	Dec 3		Advance party of 2 O.R. C.O's proceeded to HAMELINCOURT hut ref S.89.d.9.6. The remainder of the unit moved to billets in Lindsay.	JFRR
HAMELINCOURT	Dec 4		Capt WESTLAKE reported for Anaesthetic duty	JFRR
	Dec 5		Capt WESTLAKE + Lt. LOFTUS and party proceeded to A.D.S. at ST LEGER	JFRR
			Capt MORTON reported for duty	JFRR
			Capt GAFFIKIN proceeded to A.D.S. ST LEGER	JFRR
	Dec 6		Lt LOFTUS to A.D.S. CROISELLES (T.28.d.3.9.)	JFRR
			Capt HUDSON + Lt. WESTON left for Lonsdorp Camp J.F. CROSS F.E.C. ROBINSON RAMC	
	Dec 7		Proceeding on leave	
			Advanced Dressing Stations opened in town of St Leger	
	Dec 8		Three unposted RAMC reported for duty at	
	Dec 9		In view of deeply being driver active problems being anticipated the bearer section of the unit was augmented by two from 137 Field Ambulance	
	Dec 10		CAPTAIN J CRAWFORD MC RAMC (135 F.A.) attached for temporary duty	
	Dec 11		LT C.J. BUCKLEY M.O.R.E. (R.A.F.) reported for temporary duty from 137 F.A.	
			21 O.R.s RAMC reported for temporary duty from 137 F.M. Co.	
	Dec 12		LT E.J. BUCKLEY reported for duty at HENIN POST dressing station T.9t.9.9.5.1.8 in rear of the wire	
			7 OR from 137 F.M. 136 R.A.F. reported for temporary duty from 137 F.A.	
	Dec 13		Capt J.C. CRAWFORD M.C. departed & temporary duty returning Lt MacGREGOR	
			Capt WESTLAKE proceeded on leave	
			Unit kept to work along of re-subregation of attached C.M. being on the Divisional Front. The O.R.S. 3	
			have orders over arrangement all necessary preventation with the	

Army Form C. 2118.

WAR DIARY
or
INTELLIGENCE SUMMARY

(Erase heading not required.)

136 Field Ambulance
40th Division

Army Reference France S1.0
S.B.

Instructions regarding War Diaries and Intelligence Summaries are contained in F. S. Regs., Part II. and the Staff Manual respectively. Title Pages will be prepared in manuscript.

Place	Date	Hour	Summary of Events and Information	Remarks and references to Appendices
HAZEBROUCK	Dec 14		CAPT J.C. CRAWFORD M.B. returned from Temporary duty 135 F.A. & 135 Field Ambulance reported to Temporary duty	
	Dec 16		Post run from 136 Field Ambulance to Armentières & reconnoitred with necessary of 9th Regt and Section of 135 F.A. Kept went	
			& 135 F.A. 136 Kept went section 9th Kept went	
	Dec 17		W.O.R., 9/135 Field Ambulance attached returned to their respective units	
			CAPT E.J. MORETON R.A.M.C. posted to 40th D.A.C. a Class B attached. CAPT D. CRELLIN reported for duty. Oth. & 7LT	
			CAPT CRELLIN A.M. to charge at A.D.S. CROISELLES & relieving 9 LT. I. WESTLAKE who relieved P.A.L. go 7	
	Dec 20		1 N.C.O. & 8 O.Rs. medical orderly untied	
	Dec 21		CAPT P.J. GAFFIKIN detached to Temporary duty with Heavy Artillery. CAPT R.C. HEWITT returned from duty at 21 C.C.S	
			LT R.E. BERNEY	
	Dec 23		LT. SHENKEY admitted to hospital a wounded case. CAPT R.C. HEWITT departed to duty with DIST Army	
			Lt. R.C.H.R. ROBINSON returned from leave a duties near the command to 7-4-17	
	Dec 26		LT. J.C. LOFFUE reported for Temporary duty as R.M.O. 18th WELSH REGT. MAJOR C.B. BRETT	
			LT. F.L. STONE R.E. U.S.A. reported for Temporary duty	
	Dec 27		The R.A.P. & Bearer Post at QUARRY (T.16.b.9.4) & A.D.S. CROISELLES handed over to a Field Ambulance 7 34th Div.	
			CAPTAIN CRELLIN in inspection returning to New Helper	
	Dec 29		CAPTAIN WESTLAKE returned from leave a departed for duty with 40 Div. R.E. 10A	
	Dec 31		MAJOR BARRETT & LT. STONE departed after 7 days Temporary duty	

J.R. Wellwitts
Capt
O.C. 136 Field Ambulance

COMMITTEE
MEDICAL HISTORY OF THE WAR

Date -4 MAR 1918

WAR DIARY or INTELLIGENCE SUMMARY

Army Form C. 2118

VOLUME XX Page I.

136 Fd Amb

Map Reference 5.18

Place	Date	Hour	Summary of Events and Information	Remarks and references to Appendices
HAMELINCOURT S29 d9 b	1/2/18		1 O.R. detailed for temporary duty at 45 C.C.S. 4 O.R's (from Britain) reinforcements reported for duty	
	3/1/18		CAPTAIN D. CRELLIN R.A.M.C. deputed to A.D.S. ST LEGER nes	
	4/1/18		CAPTAIN R.C. HEWITT R.A.M.C. proceeded on 14 days leave to United Kingdom nes	
	6/1/18		One complete kit extraneous detailed for duty at 45 C.C.S. nes CAPT. P.J. GAFFIKIN M.C. returned to H.d.qrs. Handed over temporary command to CAPT. P.J. GAFFIKIN M.C.	J.R. Huddleston Capt. O.C. 136 FIELD AMBULANCE
	7-1-18	6 pm	7 O.R. R.A.M.C. reported for duty to Tulloch on strength	Capt P. Gaufford attached as R.M.O. 18 Welsh Regt. B'n
	11-1-18		2 LT J.L. LOFTUS M.U.R.C. U.S.A. attached to H.Q. from temporary duty from Tulloch on strength	
	14-1-18		1 O.R (groom batman) reported for duty for duty from 49 Div.	
			Capt H. RIVERS POLLOCK R.A.M.C. reported for duty until 49 Div.	
	15.1.18		LT J.L. LOFTUS M.U.R.C. U.S.A. definitely for temporary duty as R.M.O. 13 E. SURREY REGT. B'n	
	17.1.18		LT DE BERNEY definitely for temporary duty as R.M.O. to V.K. B'n	
	18-1-18		CAPT R.C. HEWITT R.A.M.C. returned from leave to U.K. & assumes command	P.J. Gaufford Capt R.A.M.C.
	22-1-18		LT-COL J.R. HUDLESTON R.A.M.C. returned from leave	
	23-1-18		Resumed command of the Unit.	J.R. Huddleston Lt.Col R.A.M.C. O.C. 136 F. Amb
	24-1-18		The temp was verified the nominal rolls by D.M.S. 1/2 div army nes	
	25-1-18		CAPT P.J. GAFFIKIN M.C. deputed to H.d.qrs leave nes	

Army Form C. 2118

WAR DIARY
or
INTELLIGENCE SUMMARY

Volume *** Secret
Page iii

(Erase heading not required.)

Instructions regarding War Diaries and Intelligence Summaries are contained in F. S. Regs., Part II. and the Staff Manual respectively. Title Pages will be prepared in manuscript.

Place	Date	Hour	Summary of Events and Information	Remarks and references to Appendices
Hondencourt S29 d 9.6	28/10		Enemy aircraft very active between 7pm & midnight. Saved searchlights & shuttles & covered up way.	
	31/10		CAPT. H R POLLOCK proceeded to XIth Corps / A.D.S. STEEGER (T.27.d.5.6) i relief of CAPT. D. CRELLIN who returned to these Hdqrs. CAPT. R.C. HEWITT proceeded to return CAPT BINGHAM attached 176 Bde R.F.A.	
			J R Middleton Lt Col R.A.M.C. D.C. 136 Field Ambulance	

Feb. 1918.

40/2784

1 D. 136. F. A.

WAR DIARY or INTELLIGENCE SUMMARY

Army Form C. 2118

136 Fd Amb
Volume XH
Part I
Maps 57c & 57B

Place	Date	Hour	Summary of Events and Information	Remarks and references to Appendices
HAMELINCOURT 57c Q.6 (51.B)	5/2/18		CAPT CRELLIN departed for troops duty and 3rd Batt Middlesex	
	6/2/18		LT E.M.BANKS MORC (137 FA) reported for temp'y duty. WDy	
	6/2/18		CAPT R.C. HEWITT departed to duty with A D M S MARSEILLES as about 27th ch of M WDy	
	11/2/18		LIEUTS C.O HAMILTON & ON LA ROTUNDA posted for duty & tkn in ch of f	
	12/2/18		LIEUT C.O HAMILTON procd to BLAIREVILLE (51C X6H F3) & tch in advance party? Coml WDy	
			Handed on conf at HAMELINCOURT & 2/13 N MIDLAND FIELD AMBULANCE	
			Unit moved to BLAIREVILLE WDy	
BLAIREVILLE (X 4d F.2) 51 C	15/2/18		CAPT CRELLIN proceded a leave to United Kingdom WDy	
	17/2/18		CAPT. P J GAFFIKEN returns from leave WDy	
	20/2/18		LIEUT HAMILTON proceeded to allied course at Third Army School Sanitation WDy	
	21/2/18		CAPT MACGREGOR (ad - hyfad) posted for ch of	
	23/2/18		LIEUT LAKER M.O.R.C posted for duty (temporary attached to 137 FA. LIEUT DE BERNEY otsd to ch of f WDy	
	24/2/18		CAPT R RIVERS POLLOCK posted a tkn LIEUT LA ROTUNDA to 137 FA, temp'y duty WDy	
			CAPT R D MACGREGOR otsd to ch of f	

J R Hullett
Lieut-Col
O.C. 136 Fd Amb

160/2900

136th Field Ambulance.

April 1918

COMMITTEE FOR THE
OFFICIAL HISTORY OF THE WAR
Date 6 JUN 1918

WAR DIARY or INTELLIGENCE SUMMARY

Army Form C. 2118

136 Field Ambulance

Volume XXII, Part I

Sheets 57c, 51c, 51B
Maps 57D
LENS 1/10000 rd

Place	Date	Hour	Summary of Events and Information	Remarks and references to Appendices
BLAIREVILLE 51c 44 c 9.5.	1/3/16		17 O.R. detached for temporary duty at 45 C.C.S. returned to Unit. Major 24 O.R. detached for temporary duty at 23 C.C.S. returned to Unit. Major	
	3/3/16		LIEUT. HAMILTON, M.D.R.C. returned to Major	
	4/3/16		CAPT CRELLIN returned from leave. Major	
	6/3/16		CAPT J CRAWFORD M.C. reported for duty. LIEUT LA ROTONDA, M.R.C. attached for duty. CAPT P.J. GAFFIKIN M.C.	
	7/3/16		CAPT J CRAWFORD M.C. & 4 o.rks attached in lieu of 9 O.Rks Major	
	9/3/16		40 O.R. RAMC Order 414 received. Major	
	10/3/16		Alteration to A.B. 30 received Major	
	11/3/16		CAPT POLLOCK returned from leave at 11th Fld Amb C.C.S. attached. LIEUT EUBANKS M.D.R.C. reported 137 FA Major	
	12/3/16		20 O.R. reinforcements posted for duty. Major	
	13/3/16		LIEUT LANES reported for duty. Left for 2 days Corps School Station Major	
	14/3/16		1 O.R. reinforcement reported for duty. Major	
	15/3/16		1 N.C.O. reinforcement reported for duty. Major	
	16/3/16		LIEUT HAMILTON detached to temporary duty at R.M.O. 2/1st Batt Major	
	17/3/16		MAJOR CRAWFORD M.C. proceeded on leave Major	
	19/3/16		4 O.R. to R.A.M.C. Dr. 56 returned. Major	
	20/3/16		Rect returned F.Std. List 5/15/1.2. MAJOR GAFFIKIN & 36 OR reported at B..d Amb open dressing Stat. adjacent to A.M.D.S. HAMELINGCOURT(57c D.99. d.963) at	
	21/3/16		CAPT CRELLIN 0/1/3 R/c detailed to report to MAJOR GAFFIKIN at A.M.D.S. HAMELINGCOURT (57c a 23 central) Major	
	22/3/16		4/- Wounded ranks & 1 person Major loaded by ambulance car sent to LAYETTE. Evacuated to Railway Junction.	
AYETTE 57 D F.11 b.9.1.	23/3/16		Authority Revel Barony ... at Ayette M9 Out word of LAYETTE(57D F.11 b.9.1) Army F.1 309 - WFA started no. at 10 a.m. — F.9.5 and R.C. 137 FA at 9.1.M. Evac FA (57 a 23 central.) 3 Road stretcher and 4 M.BR HAMELINCOURT M94	

Army Form C. 2118

WAR DIARY
or
INTELLIGENCE SUMMARY

136 Field Ambulance

PAGE 2

(Erase heading not required.)

Instructions regarding War Diaries and Intelligence Summaries are contained in F.S. Regs, Part II. and the Staff Manual respectively. Title Pages will be prepared in manuscript.

Place	Date	Hour	Summary of Events and Information	Remarks and references to Appendices
AYETTE 37D F6 C9.1	24/3/18		S.B.S., a B advl.? Bttns. at GOMIECOURT	
BUCQUOY 37D C11.a.8.0	24/3/18		Unit withdrew and to Coy BUCQUOY (37D C11.a.8.0) arriving at 10.30 a.m.	
MONCHY-AU-BOIS 57D E.6 & 9.6	25/3/18 26/3/18		Arrived at MONCHY-AU-BOIS arriving at 3 a.m. Am. Dressing Station opened & Bearer in readiness to be near wounded at 3.30 a.m. Wounded commenced to arrive at 4.30 a.m. Heavy gunfire. Unit on to evening. Unit (136 Field Ambulance) at midnight. Unit to move to POMMIER	
POMMIER 57C b3.a.6.7	26/3/18	11 a.m.	Moved. Unit ordered to shift E. Moved at 11.30 p.m. to HABARCQ	
HABARCQ 51C K.f.c2.8	27/3/18	5.30 a.m.	Moved. Ordered to move across to SOMBRIN	
SOMBRIN 51C O25 t.4.6	27/3/18	4.30 p.m.	Moved	
	28/3/18		Evacn of Injury Cases in INCB 4/cars reported missing	
	29/3/18		Unit moved at 9.30 a.m. to BAJUS	
BAJUS Lens A 19194	29/3/18	3.30 p.m.	Moved	
IF 81	30/3/18		Majr. P.J. GAFFIKIN N.E. deputed for duty to 49th Division for duty as D.A.D.M.S. Lt LAUER deputed for duty and 13th Batt. for to-day	

J.R. Bladderton
Lt Col RAMC
O.C. 136 F Ambulance

1875 Wt: W593/826 1,000,000 4/15 J.B.C. & A. A.D.S.S./Forms/C. 2118.

140/2900

136th Field Ambulance

Apr 19.18

COMMITTEE FOR THE
MEDICAL HISTORY OF THE WAR
Date 6 JUL 1918

WAR DIARY or INTELLIGENCE SUMMARY

Army Form C. 2118

136 Fd Amb

Place	Date	Hour	Summary of Events and Information	Remarks and references to Appendices
BAJUS (LENS 17E)	1/4/18		Unit moved from BAJUS to ARLIN (CARDS JUNCTION) entraining for MERVILLE detrained & marched	
SAILLY-SUR-LA-LYS	2nd		to SAILLY-SUR-LA-LYS (Sheet 36 G7A 7.3) WA	
LA LYS	3rd		Unit established H.Qrs at M.D.S. SAILLY-SUR-LA-LYS during all walkers from Divisional Front	
S.G.7.A.7.3 Sht 36	5th		CAPT ALLAN taken a change but temporarily attached to 135 Sn station for duty. WA	
	7th		MAJOR H. W. BRUCE reported for duty. WA	
			A.D.S. 3 Beam Posts (Right Brigade) taken on from O.C. 137 F.A. and No 3 S. F. CRAWFORD M.C., MAJOR H.W. BRUCE & CAPTAIN H RIVERS POLLOCK & 370 O.R's supplied for duty at A.D.S. & Posts	
	9d		CAPTAIN G. MORRIS reported for duty. WA	
		4 a.m.	Got 4 a.m. long range shell fire	
		6 a.m.	sent into ambulance ord 1 A.D.S.	
		6 a.m.	shelling increased. St Venues shops shelled A.D.S. shelled	
		9 a.m.	shell damage known not A.D.S. 3 HORSED AMBULANCE reported at O.C. 137 F.A.	
		10.15 a.m.	Man. Jones S.M. wounded at ADJ MAJOR CRAWFORD + CAPT POLLOCK	
		11.30 a.m.	Unit Hdqrs advanced to DOULIEU (36a F30 c.6.6.) William wounded whilst 2nd at harn.	
DOULIEU			MAJOR ORME & CAPT POLLOCK returned from DOULIEU & VIEUX BERQUIN & VIEUX BERQUIN clearing at 11 p.m. WA	
		6 p.m.	Unit Hdqrs moved from DOULIEU to VIEUX BERQUIN	
VIEUX BERQUIN 10th HAZEBROUCK 4h	10th	2 p.m.	Unit moved from VIEUX BERQUIN to STRAZEELE arriving at 4.30 p.m. & opened a M.D.S. at 5 p.m. & then moved WA	
STRAZEELE	11th		M.D.S. taken on by O.C. 94 th F.A.M. established here. On being relieved unit moved to BORRE (HAZEBROUCK 4 G)	
			MAJOR CRAWFORD & CAPT CRELLIN & Bearers returned to Hdqrs. WA	
BORRE	12th		Unit moved from BORRE to HONDEGHEM, Emergency MDS on motor run up from HAZEBROUCK 3G. Bearers division attached to	
HONDEGHEM	13d		Unit moved to STAPLES. (HAZEBROUCK 3F) WA	

WAR DIARY
or
INTELLIGENCE SUMMARY

(Erase heading not required.)

Army Form C. 2118

Page II

Instructions regarding War Diaries and Intelligence Summaries are contained in F. S. Regs., Part II. and the Staff Manual respectively. Title Pages will be prepared in manuscript.

Place	Date	Hour	Summary of Events and Information	Remarks and references to Appendices
STAPLE	14th		Unit moved from STAPLE to TILQUES (HAZEBROUCK 3C) May	
TILQUES	16th		CAPTAIN POLLOCK posted to duty with 1/1st Middlesex Regt May	
	17th		LIEUT HAMILTON posted to duty and 13th E Jarret Regt	
			14 O R's reinforcements reported for duty	
	18th		LIEUT HAMILTON 2d exchange again a rent with 1/0 R's & Temporary duty with 137 F. Amb. By	
	19th		CAPT CRELLIN posted to duty with 2/4 Middlesex Regt	
			1 OR reinforcement reported to duty	
	21st		Unit moved from TILQUES to BOISDINGHEM (HAZEBROUCK B3 4.1)	
BOISDINGHEM	22nd		CAPT ALLAN posted to duty as IV Corps Reinforcement Camp May	
			CAPT GREEN reported to duty including 11 men returned from temporary duty at SUCCES By	
	26th		2 O R's nursing interned P.O.W. as 2nd M ??? Hy	
	27th		Unit stand to "STAND TO" MAJOR W 6.P. McKNIGHT CAPT ALLINSON & LIEUT McALOON reported to duty temporary from 13? F. stables —	
			LIEUT McALOON posted to duty at 13th East Surrey Regt May	
	30th		Unit moved from BOISDINGHEM to ST. MOMELIN (HAZEBROUCK 6A, 3D) May	

I. R. Hamilton
Col. R.A.M.C.
O.C. 138 Field Ambulance

140/2983.

No. 136 J.A.

COMMITTEE FOR THE
MEDICAL HISTORY OF THE WAR
Date 9 JUL 1918

A.D.M.S. **Secret** 16th Divn. No. A.533.
40th Division.

Herewith War Diary of 136th Field Ambulance for month of May 1918.

War Diary of 135th Field Ambulance has been sent direct to you by that unit.

Headquarters,
16th Divn.
4th June 1918.

RN Greenwood
hy- DADS
Lieut-Colonel.
A.A. & Q.M.G., 16th Division.

Anoth Div

2

Forwarded.
A.D.M.S. 40th Divn

7/6/18

A.D.M.S.
40th DIVISION
No. 159/ty
Date 7-6-18.

WAR DIARY or INTELLIGENCE SUMMARY

Army Form C. 2118

136 3rd Cdn [?]
Scale Maps Hazebrouck
27
13 Salowe

Vol 24

VOLUME XXIV
SHEET 1

Place	Date	Hour	Summary of Events and Information	Remarks and references to Appendices
ST. MOMELIN	1-5-18		Unit moved at 9 a.m. to WEMAERS CAPPEL (Reference 3.F.)	
WAEMERS CAPPEL	2-5-18		Unit moved at 71 m. E ST. MOMELIN (Reference 3.D)	
	4-5-18		Holiday detail paraded & M.69009 Pte W. FOSTER & M/139211 Pte E. JOHNSON (A.S.C. MT.) slong w/ a 2 mule team departed on duty w/ S.M.T.O. IX Corps	
			MAJOR W.R.P. McNEIGHT [struck through] returned to 136 F. Amb. from	
			CAPT. ALLINSON WARD SMITH, MORRIS & GREEN posted for duty w/ A.D.M.S. 29th Div	
			LIEUT. HAMILTON posted for duty w/ O.C. A.D.M.S. 33rd Div [remain???]	
	7-5-18		Two N.C.O reprimanded reported for duty. RC	
	10-5-18		MAJOR CRAWFORD of 3.O.R. a.d. km outdoor by motor for duty at artillery att'd MAP ungun	
	14-5-18		Paraded a 14 days apparel hands drilled from hospital dept + MAJOR H.W. BRUCE. ???	
	14.5.18		Took over Expiry charge from Lt Col J.R. Huddleston. NbBS. IR to block trucks-- 6	
	18.5.18		Medical Board convened to No. 69557 Pte Whitehead J.W., M. 3704 Pte Martin J.T. R. AMC and M12/051407 OLL Gradstore R. A.S.C. MT. net	
	28.5.18		136 Field Ambulance Touring Cab coming of 2 Officers, 1 W.O. 6 N.C.O.S and 15 O.R.s with 6 Transport + equipment moved at 9 am to Suvreton (Reference 4.B port.S.A.). Running formed [2 words] 2 Officer, 14 N.C.O.s + 109 O.R.s transferred to 137 F.A. Motor ambulance temporarily attached to S.M.T.O. 11s Corps retained to Hdqns w/H. Touring Cab moved to Enquin G.E.	
	29.5.18		Handed over charge to Lt Col J.R. Huddleston to which its base sub.[?] Hutheson now Reported.	

1875. Wt. W593/826 1,000,000 4/15 J.B.C. & A. A.D.S.S./Forms/C. 2118.

WAR DIARY
or
INTELLIGENCE SUMMARY

(Erase heading not required.)

Army Form C. 2118

Instructions regarding War Diaries and Intelligence Summaries are contained in F. S. Regs., Part II. and the Staff Manual respectively. Title Pages will be prepared in manuscript.

Sheet II

Place	Date	Hour	Summary of Events and Information	Remarks and references to Appendices
ENQUIN LE (CHEMIN)	30-6-17		Returned from leave & took over command from Major B W BEATY 104 O.R.a Enquiny started & 137 F. ambce returned. MAJOR CRAWFORD arrived & 137 F. Amb. Unit nos. ascertained of A.D.M.S. 11th Division. I R Hadden Col R.a.m.c O.C. 136 Field Ambulance	

M.O/3076.

1367 4.G.

June 1918.

COMMITTEE FOR THE
MEDICAL HISTORY OF THE WAR
Date 7 AUG 1918

Secret - 136 2nd Aug
Army Form C. 2118
136 F Amb

WAR DIARY or INTELLIGENCE SUMMARY

(Erase heading not required.)

Vol XXV
Sht 1

Place	Date	Hour	Summary of Events and Information	Remarks and references to Appendices
ENQUIN SUR BAILLON	1/6/18		Main Dressing Station established for the reception of sick in conjunction with 7 Canadian	
Colln 13 BD	3/6/18		7 eval from 4th Shermen Division Wdy	
	4/6/18		3 NCO's reported Hdqrs from 137 F Amb Wdy	
			MAJOR CRAWFORD MC, relinquished to hospital & evacuated to M & B. R.C.S. Two trained motorcars & one motor ambulance detailed to Turquay Hqrs and 4th Sherwen Division during march. Returning 7 same day.	
	9/6/18		1 P.B. Soldier reported to duty. 2 OR's reported to 137 F. Amb. OO 2 R's attended 7 days at Cadet camp at ENQUIN (60th Sherwen Division) Wdy	
	15/6/18		10 R reported Hdqrs from 137 F Amb. MAJOR CRAWFORD reported for temporary duty	
	19/6/18		Unit came on the establishment of ADMS 34th DIV.	
	20/6/18		Medical Board recommended re-classifying P.B. joining Wdy later moving date to men to another area	
	21/6/18		Sick and evacs evacuated attended 2 duty funerary Clerk closed Wdy	
	22/6/18		1 P.B. soldier applied to duty Wdy	
	24/6/18		Ech'd relief on 4th 103 F Solders. Unit moved from ENQUIN & LART with vehicles	
			4 "Sherwen" MA	
LART	25/6/18		Unit moved from LART to EBBLINGHEM Wdy	
HAZEBROUCK				
SA-LA				
EBBLINGHEM	28/6/18		Main Sherwen Ch'ch opened from 119th & 120th Brigades Wdy	
Sht 27 T/5067	29/6/18		ADS team opened a RAP and acted as a scheme for rearrangement made I.R. Shields O.C. 136 Field Amb Lt Col for	

1875 Wt. W593/826 1,000,000 4/15 J.B.C. & A. A.D.S.S./Forms/C. 2118.

Army Form C. 2118

136th Fd Amb
Secret
Map Sheet 27

WAR DIARY
or
INTELLIGENCE SUMMARY
(Erase heading not required.)

VOLUME XXVI Sheet 1

Place	Date	Hour	Summary of Events and Information	Remarks and references to Appendices
EBBLINGHEM T18 d 2.7	1-7-18		Main Dressing Station for 119th & 120th Inf Brigades	
	3-7-18		CAPT T J BUCKLEY R.a.m.C reported for duty & is taken on the strength	
	4-7-18		CAPT L J PILBEAM (Dental Officer) temporarily attached for duty also taken on the strength for return to his unit at time of expiry	
	6-7-18		Temp 2 Mr o Hon LIEUT. GOODLEY A.S. Bon CAPT. (L.L. Gazette 26.7.18)	
	9-7-18		LIEUT W WIGGINS LIEUT W STONER } M.o.RC USA reported for duty LIEUT C MARTIN	
	11-7-18		CAPT. L Mr GOODLEY proceeded on leave CAPT PELLIER detached as Surgeon R.M.O. to 13th Bn. E. LANCS. O	
	12-7-18		100 O.R.s reinforcements reported for duty	
	16-7-18		1 Sgt (M.T.) reinforcement reported for duty	
	17-7-18		CAPT PELLIER returned to H.Q.s from Regiment duty	
	19-7-18		119th Inf Bgde detailed to 1st AUSTRALIAN DIVISION. Sick and wounded from M.D.S. handed over to the	
	20-7-18		260 O.R.s reinforcements reported for duty	
	24-7-18		M.O. (Lieut A L Last) gassed accidentally not to exceed 50	
	27-7-18		CAPT L Mr GOODLEY returned from leave	
	29-7-18		1 N.C.O reported for duty	
	31-7-18		M.D.S. admissions during month 73 " " remaining in hospital 43 " " evacuated during month O.R. 10 O.R. 598 " " " " O.R. 9 O.R. 216 " " " " to duty O.R. 9 O.R. 382	J R Nicholls Lt Col Ra C OC 136 Fd Ambulance

140/3200.

126 M 7.A.

WAR DIARY
or
INTELLIGENCE SUMMARY

Army Form C. 2118

Volume XXVII
Page I

136 Field Ambulance

Place	Date	Hour	Summary of Events and Information	Remarks and references to Appendices
EBBLINGHEM	1/8/18		Major Kearney Station for 119 & 120 Inf Bdes. WDy	
	3/8/18		Lt Wiggins MORC & Lt Stiner MORC attached for duty. WDy	
	5/8/18		Capt Buckley RAMC granted 10 days agricultural leave to the United Kingdom WDy	
	6/8/18		Unit had 2nd Army Show and Infantry Costs and accommodation for 50 patients. Supply 120 Inf Bgd Unit L137 Field. Capt McLeod RAMC discharged attached for temporary duty WDy	
	14/8/18		10 R dated W attacked Infy Bn wounded cases. WDy	
	15/8/18		10 R shower baths Cap attached for temporary duty	
	18/8/18		10 R (WIC #7) attached. W Infy attached. WDy	
	20/8/18		Accommodation in Infantry Costs increased to 250 beds. WDy	
	21/8/18		Unit received 6 Corps Commdrs WDy.	
			The Divisional relieved 30th to 4th Div. RAMC n.a. and 7th Div. were later recovered from the front.	
	23/8/18		Divisional attended Field and 100 beds transferred to 35 F Amb. 2 O.R's requisite supplies to duty. Brass funds a little attention received to duty 1 Pte 136 Fld Amb	
	24/8/18		Lt Wiggins attached Hygiene Ofr. Temp. duty turned over. Received On-boat No 186/50d 137 Fld Amb.	
	28/8/18		Capt Buckley returned from leave. One ford car attached A ADMS for duty. Gen'l Bde Emergency d 137 Field Amb	
	29/8/18		Capt Buckley posted as RMO to 8 Ber Welsh Regt. 311 of 6/6 WDy	
			7/Sgt W Partick transferred to 42 Field Amb WDy	
	30/8/18		On Aug 12 J. R's and 1 Water Transport provided 1 cook at 36/CSS for duty turned on out	
WALLON CAPPEL 36A/CCS9	31/8/18	7/-	Unit moved from bus here by Mns in 30 R's	
			Sick summary 1-8-18 Officers ad O.R 43	
			Admitted sick unfit 5 " " 74 " 324	
			Discharged	
			Remaining 31-8-18 1610 R's 1bely 75 granted	

J R Mellestin
O.C 136 Field Ambulance

140/3259

Sept 1918.

136. F. Amb

COMMITTEE FOR THE
MEDICAL HISTORY
Date 9 NOV

WAR DIARY / INTELLIGENCE SUMMARY

Army Form C. 2118

Volume XXVII

Sent. 136 [signatures] 36A / 27... / 28

Place	Date	Hour	Summary of Events and Information	Remarks and references to Appendices
WALLON CAPPEL 36A/C5a59	1-9-18		Unit continuing its General Post Station. CAPT PILBEAM (R.A.M.C. Surgeon) attached for temporary duty. 1 NCO reported for duty, also a WO attached at EGGLINGHEM dept. on admin. & sports details.	
	3-9-18		LT. MARTIN MORR. a 30 R's to the Unite for course of instruction.	
	4-9-18		MAJOR CRAWFORD & CAPT HOWARD + 36 OR's unit on active employ't & transport left Nº ?? 1	
			Wallace Man. Dressing Station at 36A/F50 C57	
	6-9-18		MAIN Dressing Stn opened & Post Unit closed.	
	7-9-18		MAIN DRESSING STATION moved to 36A/F 29 d 8.9. Map	
	8-9-18		Unite moved to Main Dressing Station. Staff of 2nd employ at BRITANNIA FARM. LT MARTIN & 7 OR's moved to WALLON CAPPEL for attachm of 3 and 7 Brigade reserve. CAPT PILBEAM attd. M admin staff.	
36A/F29 d69	10-9-18		LIEUT WIGGINS detached for duty at Sports Cub. 1 return MAJOR H. Nº BRUCE proceed on leave.	
	12-9-18		Distribut'n of Sports between employment of 1 NCO & 40R's to 40Nº a 7OR's to WALLON CAPPEL LT MARTIN return to H.Q.	
			LT STONER reported to temp duty with 135 F.amb. Map	
	14-9-18		Two units went on temp duty with 100 M.S. G return.	
	15-9-18		Mr Gray SSI. Went on to 137 Field section on duty and moved to LA BRIELLE FARM 36A/25a59 Orders to Sgts ??	
LA BRIELLE FARM 36A/L5a5.B	19-9-18		Unit moved to BRIELLE CAMP PROVEN 27/E6d. CAPT PELTIER, LT WIGGINS and 33 OR's registered help. Details of duty at H.Q. Corps Map	
PROVEN 27/E6d			Unit moved to WELSH FARM. 28/B14 c5. J.B.C. &A. A.D.S.S. Intervening at 36A/A22 d 3 6. Map	

Army Form C. 2118

WAR DIARY
or
INTELLIGENCE SUMMARY

(Erase heading not required.)

VOLUME XXVIII
Sheet II

Secret

Place	Date	Hour	Summary of Events and Information	Remarks and references to Appendices
WELSH FARM 26/B/4 C.C.S.	21-9-18		Received orders for 14th Corps to form a Misc Enemy Unit at this set to prepare ? receiving at out a model of 76 AFA Brigade & 37th Batt'n let to Belgian Army, VAR.	
	23-9-18		LT WIGGINS mounted and VBy	
	24-9-18		Evacuate column of wounded. For this purpose men drawn out 3 centres	
			CAPT HOWARD & 11 O.R.'s proceeded to SMISKE Sect 20/T n d 7,3 & no bays ambulance car to collect from NORTHERN sector.	
			LT MARTIN & 11 O.R.'s proceeded to GREEN HILL 26/C1 a 9,9 & collect from middle sector	
			LT STONER & 20 O.R.'s proceeded to BRIDGE 4 ELVERFARM 26/C 25 a 39 acting also as ty station	
			for walking from S. sector Sect. WBy	
	26-9-18		One horsed ambulance away. 2 B.R.'s proceeded to PARATONERRE FARM 20/T 26 d 2 5. & prepare ? catching my casualty walking wounded from Fr.M. Boltham & the area.	
	28-9-18	2.30 am	MAJOR R.H.M. BRACE returned from leave.	
			Misc. Garden begun. 6 mile terrain captured VBy walking wounded. 1 lorry sent to cross the nature & turn HQtrs Sent for dining supply conduct the Corps walking wounded HQtrs	
			Very few casualties VBy	
	29-9-18		Ambulance at advance that pits are established on platoon model with 28+5.S.0 RAPAT 26 + 6	36+6, 33+,
			situated at the ... dict put at M 28 a S.S + RAPAT V.1.3.a 1.9. South lists sent put at 222.c.1.9. & RAPAT HAS 7	APATCH A.S. 33- 35
			the post whs known relation to 5 N.T.B. than we 7 we nn ry 7 nd pm traveling state horsed ambulance My 28	35
	30-9-18		Sent to ASC advance	
			Total no 7 casualties min 21/9/18. Approx 3 O.R's 75,	
			H.B. for the month. Set. Approx 7 O.R's 405 O.R's 405 all T.C.C.S.	
			Wounded Approx 7 O.R's 223	
			Sick Franks TAAFO & returned at Aug 390	

J R Dunklinton
Lt Col R A M 136 Field Ambulance
O.C. 136

14/93-4

BWI + O

Cut 10/8

WAR DIARY or INTELLIGENCE SUMMARY

Army Form C. 2118

Volume XIX
136 Field Ambulance
Sent. Maps 20, 28, 36, 37

Place	Date	Hour	Summary of Events and Information	Remarks and references to Appendices
WELSH FARM 30/B.14.c.0.5	1/10/18		Unit functioning as a Main Dressing Station for wounded from initially Brigade but & Belgium troops	
		2.30pm	LT. STONER with personnel & equipment ordered for further duty. LT MARTIN and personnel, transport & equipment ordered for the middle watch.	
			The Units work on active evacuating Posts are as follows: Own at 30/D.2.8.6.6.0 & a relay post at 31.6. central. Cd. STJ at 31.B.6.5.5.	
			J. recalled to dy HQ.	
	2/10/18		MAJOR J CRAWFORD returned to 136 FA from 2 U.K. Two casualties during 24 Hrs	
	3/10/18		CAPT HOWARD returned from Strike Sch. via TC II #35 & ES being mind had J. at hen Hdy	
	4/10/18		Received orders to fall in & stand to.	
	5/10/18		Unit moved to BALLANCE CAMP PROVEN.	
	6/11/18		MAJOR H. BENZIE presiding for 7 days leave — PARIS.	
	7/10/18		Received temporary command during the absence of Lt Col. I R. HAMILTON on leave. Distinct visits to Route Distinct Mountmark Tower & more	
			Unit at the disposal of XV Corps.	
			Unit moves from Putzburg Camp, PROVEN to Main Dressing Station at 36/A.37 & 5.5 relieving 137 Field Ambulance west	
STEENWERCK 10/11/18			1 NCO & 5 men detailed to ADS (Trestle) in relief of detachment of 137 Field Ambulance sent	
36/A 37 & 5.5	11/10/18		1 Sgt, 2 cpls & 16 men detailed to Civil Hospital Armentières to prepare the site for a Main Dressing Station now	
	12/10/18		Detachment at ADS (Trestle) rejoined Unit on relief by 135 Field Ambulance soon	
	13/10/18		Handed over to Lt Col I R HAMILTON on his return from leave	
	14/10/18		LT STONER detailed to Company dy pending his return to "Rest" until E/Offr	
	15/10/18		MAJOR H W BARR with an advance party will proceed to Hospital award E CIVIL HOSPITAL ARMENTIERES	
			from an Army etc. Hy	
	16/11/18		MDS Opened at ARMENTIERES 36/B.30.c.S.2. MAJOR J CRAWFORD MC admitted Lt. t. disability Cure	

WAR DIARY or INTELLIGENCE SUMMARY

Army Form C. 2118

Volume XXIX Sect. Msp. 30
Part II 27
Page 11. 36
 37

Place	Date	Hour	Summary of Events and Information	Remarks and references to Appendices
STEENWERCK	16/10/18		Headquarters moved to Civil Hospital ARMENTIERES. Embussing as a M.O.S.S B.R.S. HQ	
ARMENTIERES 36/B20&C9	19/10/18		MAJOR J.C.RAWFORD attd. for duty to United Kingdom.	
	20/10/18		Orders received to take over from 119th Sig Troops at end of HQ	
	21/10/18		CAPT PELLIER ordered to proceed to United Kingdom	
	24/10/18		Advance party MAJOR BRUCE, CAPT HOWARD and 34 O.R's O.R.D.S. equipment proceed to WAMBRECHIES 36/E26 L.L.	
WAMBRECHIES 36/E26L2	25/10/18		MAJOR CRAWFORD & CAPT MARTIN and 360 R.a.a.R.D.J. equipment proceed to P.37/H 2 b 2) 4 Rn. A D S q	
			advance party to be known as 95 Field stationed R.a P 37/h6 & 3.2 Hq.	
	27/10/18		MAJOR BRUCE, CAPT HOWARD with personnel report at 8pm.	
			HQ moved to 37/B.19 & 44 billy in MA J S at 94 d Fosil Ambulance	
			Passing worked into a collecting unit for troops and acting to 133 F Amb (4 R C)	
37/C 19 & 44	29/10/18		R A C J another Collect material at 37/0.17 £ 6.2	
	31/10/18		Stone & reports from whoring at 11 am.	
			Lt STONER reports for temp duty	
			CAPT HOWARD granted a 14days leave at U.K. HQ	
			CAPT PELLIER attached for Supply duty and 1 R.A.M.C. arm Highlanders.	
			Strength: OR SR	
			Attached 19 368	
			Permanent 17 212 11 125	
			To Duty – 110 10 125 1 R Highlander	
			Sick – 1 1 3 – D of 95 R.A.M.C	
			End – 1 – Field Ambulance	
				D C. 136

140/3401

136 F.A.

Nov. 1918

Army Form C. 2118

WAR DIARY
or
INTELLIGENCE SUMMARY
(Erase heading not required.)

136 Field Amb

Place	Date	Hour	Summary of Events and Information	Remarks and references to Appendices
37/G.15.k.32	1/11/18		Funishing on M.D.S. and A.D.S. out 37/H.2.b.2.7	
	2/11/18		Bn bays and line from 135 F. Amb to two bays from 135 F Amb attd to 1 July 1943 10R Rwd widd wounded day	
	5/11/18		10 R. A. Bogota Hospt. Evacing duty	
	6/11/18		H Q. R. M. Q. F. to Evacing duty Hay	
	8/11/18		MDS land at 12.00 hr the moved to 37/H b wE. MDS opend at 11.00 hr ADS at 37/H.2.b.2.7 clsd at 15.30 hr & movd at 37/H.b.6.9.4 at 12.00 hrs will carry pack at 37/H.3.a.6.8	
PECQ 37/H b.u Ed	10/11/18		The Dever was out of the line. ADS clsd & not drawn & equipmt returned to Dyse day.	
			Divine moved & civilians ind 9 120 & Brigade day	
	11/11/18		MAJOR H. W. BRACE for wounded a 14 days appointed temp O.C.	
			CAPT PELLER detached for evacing duty with 12th Battn R.Irish Fusiliers	
	13/11/18		Proceeded in 14 days leave to United Kingdom. Handed on Evacing arrangement to MAJOR CRAWFORD day	

J. R. Duckworth
Lt Col. R.A.M.C.
O.C. 136 Field Ambulance

Army Form C. 2118

WAR DIARY
or
INTELLIGENCE SUMMARY
(Erase heading not required.)

Instructions regarding War Diaries and Intelligence Summaries are contained in F.S. Regs., Part II. and the Staff Manual respectively. Title Pages will be prepared in manuscript.

VOL XXX Sheet No II

SECRET Maps: Sh. 37. Sh. 36.

Place	Date	Hour	Summary of Events and Information	Remarks and references to Appendices
PECQ. 37/HCa.En7.	13/11/18 14/11/18		Assumed command. m.C. 1 NCO evacuated sick of strength. M.C.	
PT LANNOY 37/G19.2.3.2.	15/11/18		Train Dressing Station at 37/HCa central closed; Unit moved to 37/G19.B.3.2; Fixed Dressing Station. For sick of 120 BGDE. M.C. 1 NCO evacuated sick strength. M.C.	
	17/11/18 18/11/18		CAPT. HO·GOUGH RAMC taken on strength attached for duty with H.Qs. XV CORPS. M.C. Unit inspected by D.M.S. Second Army. M.C. 3 amb. cars attached from 14 M.M.C. returned to column. M.C. 2 amb. cars detailed for temp. duty with 20 M.M.C. M.C.	
	23/11/18		Orders received to move on 24-11-18 M.C.	
MOUVAUX 36/F14.d.2.4.	24/11/18		Closed Dressing Station; unit moved to 36/F14.d.2.4. M.C.	
	26/11/18		Opened XV CORPS SKIN CENTRE. M.C.	
	27/11/18		MAJOR. H.W. BRUCE returned from 14 days special leave to UK. Handed over command to MAJOR H.W. BRUCE. M. Crawford Maj. RAMC.	
	29/11/18		Assumed Express Consult. Hospital now RAMC Maj. RAMC. CpL C de C PELLIER returned from detached duty wt 132 Fld R Trns Tno Lieut Col. J.R HUDLESTON return from 14 days leave to U.K. reports	
	30/11/18 30/11/18		Handed over command to Lieut Col. J.R HUDLESTON Historical War Return Reend command. CAPT HOWARD left for Emergency duty wt 82 CCS	Admitted to unit Sick D.R. 0 0 0 R 7 2 35 6 206 Sick D.R. 22 44.6 1 26 1 26 4 2 3 22 4 2 3 Admitted to unit Killed Wounded Of 136 F.A. (wounded)

No. 136 4 A

WAR DIARY or INTELLIGENCE SUMMARY

Army Form C. 2118

Vol XXXI Sheet 1.

Place	Date	Hour	Summary of Events and Information	Remarks and references to Appendices
NOEUX & T14 d.1.3.	1-12-18		Functioned as XVth Corps Clearing Station. Patch covering Officer 1. OR's 31	
	6-12-18		Capt HOWARD detailed for Tropping duty at 61 CCS. 1 day adv'e can relieved from Tropping duty now 14 NAS	
	7-12-18		1 NCO detailed to Evey duty at General Rail WAMBRECHIES.	
	8-12-18		Sec morning rel'n detailed to Tropping duty as dysentery hospital May	
	9-12-18		Capt HOWARD return'd & reports from 61 CCS. May	
	12-12-18		3 homes 4 horses & 2 wagons attached to 14 CCS for Trav. Lt STONER & Lt MARTIN proceeded on Tropping duty & M.R May	
			Capt HOWARD evacuated as ill to 14 CCS. May	
			Lt Col HADLESTON ? on duty ADMS on 2nd Army of detail a bars. 2 CA HUMPHRY. From O.R's respective units.	
	13-12-18		1.OR R.A.C. at destroyed & 30R's R.A.C. May	
	14-12-18		1.OR R.A.C. destroyed Lt PARKER reported to 30R's R.A.C. May	
	16-12-18		1.OR R.A.C. destroyed May	
	17-12-18		1.OR R.A.C. & 1NCB & 2C.H.T. destroyed & 61 R.A.C	
	20-12-18		Lt PARKER returned & reported to England & 6 O.R's May	
	23-12-18		Lt STONER & Lt MARTIN return for home 10R reinforcement reported & duty. May	
	25-12-18		Capt & 2nd Lt GODLEY proceeded 10day leave to UK. Detailed reg home May	
	28-12-18		Lt MARTIN return'd & Tropping duty at hospital St Coup ST ANDRÉ May	
	31-12-18		1NCB R.A.C destroyed & 20R. May	
			Return reported, were OH O.R's	
			attached 1 21	
			evacuated 1CCS 15 589	
			" hospital 1 DR5 2 56	
			Total 11 439	
			Remaining 3 93	

I.R. Chudleigh
Lt Col R.A.M.C
O.C. 136 F. Ambulance

40 DIV

Box 2418

No 136 + a

136 Fd Amb
Sheet 36

Army Form C. 2118

WAR DIARY
or
INTELLIGENCE SUMMARY

(Erase heading not required.)

Vol XXXII
Sheet I

Instructions regarding War Diaries and Intelligence Summaries are contained in F. S. Regs., Part II. and the Staff Manual respectively. Title Pages will be prepared in manuscript.

Place	Date	Hour	Summary of Events and Information	Remarks and references to Appendices
MORVAUX 36T 14.d.13.	1-1-19 2-8-19 5-1-19 6-1-19 9-1-19 10-1-19 11-1-19 12-1-19 13-1-19 17-1-19 23-1-19 25-1-19 30-1-19 29-1-19		Functioning as XV Corps Clear. Centre. Patients remaining 93 [illeg.] 10R RMC & 1 PB ¿ WR of Amatady sta. 10R RM2 died & evacuated CAPT GINGT returned from leave LT STONER attached to Infantry Schools and 135 F amb. 10R attached to 31 Hypo + 20R2 with 81 reinforcement by regulars and 30R's 1 WR of Amatady sta. evan 2am W GODLEY returned from leave + 2 WR 10R attached XV Corps + 10R with 39 Stationary Hospital, 10R with reinforced by regulars and [illeg.] 7 OR & 1 WR of Amatady sta. 10R & 12 WR of Amatady sta. [illeg.] 8 horses 4 brown mule 5 T engine detailed to HQs and 40 & 81 the Train returned 1 Hypo MAJOR CRAWFORD provided a lecture down to U.R. LT BRACKET reported to Ma[jor] 1 R (MCD) evacuated sick. CAPT PELLIER provided + CAPT ALLINSON reported to Infantry Scho[ol] Patients admitted 353 Evacuated CCS 57 hospital & 9 RS 10 To duty 333 Remaining 46	V8 32 1 PD Marsh CAPT Rue OC 136 F Ambulance

No 136 Field Ambulance

WAR DIARY / INTELLIGENCE SUMMARY

136th Fd. Amb. Army Form C. 2118

WO 95/33

Map Sheet 36 Secret
Sheet No. I

Place	Date	Hour	Summary of Events and Information	Remarks and references to Appendices
MOUVAUX 36/T.14.d.1.3	1-2-19		About fourteen cases XV Corps other ranks. Patients evening 46	
	2-2-19		1.O.R. R.A.C. discharged to U.K. without a hour. CAPT ALLINSON reported for temporary duty fr 137 Fd. Amb. May	
	3-2-19		1.O.R. reported not for temporary duty with 178 Bde R.F.A.	
	4-2-19		1.O.R. reported not for temporary duty with 178 Bde R.F.A. 10R (A.S.C.M.T) evacuated sick May	
	5-2-19		1.O.R (A.S.C.M.T) & U.R.T. discharged. When Gave Brown Gazette. LT COL HUDLESTON, MC, CAPT & 2 GUDGEON, MC, 30408 Cpl May OXLEY, D.C.M. JRMC	
	6-2-19		MAJOR CRAWFORD M.C. admitted from leave May	
	7-2-19		2.O.R.'s U.R.T. discharged	
	8-2-19		CAPT ALLINSON rejoined 137 Fd Bde Amb	
	9-2-19		Undel. rem 1 MAJOR BRUCE provided a special train 4 A.R.	
	11-2-19		Arrived brought during the temporary absence of Lieut Col I.R. HUDLESTON, in leave	1 R. had attached to RAMC OC 136 F Amb attached a
	11-2-19			workhorse more reserve
	12-2-19		1 OR. transferred to Sgt. Scotts for club-- 1 (NCo) sent to hospital evacuated. 2 O.R.'s (RAMC)	2 O.R. (RAMC) discharged in U.K. 1 unit officer to U.K. North
			8 O.R. (RAMC) discharged in U.K. 1 warrant officer & 1 O.R. (RAMC) to U.K. for demobilisation some	
	12.2.15		1 OR attd to 29 Sta HD regional units MWS	
	15.2.19		1 S/Sgt. & 10.R (RAMC) to U.K. for demobilisation arm	
	16.2.19		2 Ofs. Returns & 1 Box (R.F.A. BDY) to U.K. for demobilisation to	
	17.2.19		1 Oft. (RAMC) to U.K. for demobilisation 12,50	
	20.2.19		1 nursing orderly attached to X Corp H.Qtrs. for duty 2 O.R. (R+10 H.T) decided in U.K. 2 O.R. (RAMC) demobilised	
	21.2.19		2 O.R. (R.A.O.C. MT) to U.K. for demobilisation. 2 OR (RAMC) to U.K. for demobilisation. word.	

1875 Wt. W593/826 1,000,000 4/15 J.B.C. & A. A.D.S.S./Forms/C.2118.

Army Form C. 2118

WAR DIARY
or
INTELLIGENCE SUMMARY

(Erase heading not required.)

Vol XXXII
Sheet No 11

Instructions regarding War Diaries and Intelligence Summaries are contained in F.S. Regs., Part II. and the Staff Manual respectively. Title Pages will be prepared in manuscript.

Place	Date	Hour	Summary of Events and Information	Remarks and references to Appendices
MOUVAUX	22.2.19		1 NCO sent HQ for duty at D.E.M.S. Officer 2 ORs (RAMC) to UK for demobilisation sent	
56/T/14.12	23.2.19		2 ORs (RAMC) to UK for demobilisation. Capt Major J CRAWFORD M.C. from field to 135 Field ambulance. 2 OR (RAMC) to UK for demobilisation was	
	24.2.19		Reorganization effected on hand of the admission from J CRAWFORD and OC for beyond duties here	
	26.2.19		2 ORs demobilised in UK (RAMC)	
	27.2.19		2 ORs to U.K. for demobilisation (RAMC) sent	
	28.2.19		2 ORs " " " (RAMC) Wholetimes Major R Armie	
			Transfers of Patients admitted during the month 210	
			discharged to duty 195	
			evacuated 35	
			remaining 28/2/19 31	
			Lieut Col Armie, Major R Armie	
			to 136 Field ambulance	

116/3001

17 JUL 1919

136. 7.0.

Nov. 1919

Army Form C. 2118

Sheet 36/F 14 d 10.30

Sheet I Vol XXIII

WAR DIARY or INTELLIGENCE SUMMARY
(Erase heading not required.)

Instructions regarding War Diaries and Intelligence Summaries are contained in F.S. Regs., Part II. and the Staff Manual respectively. Title Pages will be prepared in manuscript.

Place	Date	Hour	Summary of Events and Information	Remarks and references to Appendices
Movement 1919	Mar 1st		1 attack on Koufra 30 2 OR₃ (Rome) to UK for discharge	
	" 2		3 H.D (Lines) to Collecting Camp for discharge. Captain C McCallion returned from leave UK. Capt H.O. Gough proceeded on 21 days special leave to UK. XV Corps Van Column closed for the reception of sick. Capt C McC Allen + 1 OR₃ attached for duty to 11 C.C.S. Next week draw trans	
	" 3		5 H.D. Horses + 2 Mules to Collecting Camp for discharge	
	" 4		Sun Right clear of patients unless shown hot	
	" 5		Lt C.E. Martin MRC (USA) struck off strength was stopped from 26/10/15. 2 HDs + 3 Mules to Collecting Camp for discharge hot	
	" 6		3 OR₃ Rome to UK for discharge. 3 Drivers (RASC attd) transferred to no CC. GOC San Gion	
	" 7		1 OR Sgt Rome. Employer to no 10 Stationary Hospital Road 3 OR₃ (Rome) to UK for discharge. 2 OR₃ (RAMC not attd) transferred to 400bn at Fd Col (hob ford Lieut WH Stones re attached to Lord Derr section in no 1/4 town"	
	" 8		2 OR₃ Rome + 1 Driver RASC to UK for discharge	
	" 9		3 OR₃ Rome to UK for discharge	
	" 10		3 OR₃ Rome to UK for discharge	
	" 11		2 HDs + 3 Rubber + 1 Bn (RFA Italian attd) to UK for discharge hot	
	" 13		6 OR₃ Rome + 1 OR₃ Rome (?) (A.E.15) 5 OR₃ Rome to UK for discharge sent	
	" 14		1 OR₃ Rome on detached duty to UK for discharge	
	" 15		Capt CdC McCallin to UK for discharge. 2 OR₃ Rome to UK for discharge + 1 OR (Rome) erased (have sick attendance main tower at 126 Field Ambulance	

1875 Wt. W593/826 1,000,000 4/15 J.B.C. & A. A.D.S.S./Forms/C. 2118.

Army Form C. 2118

WAR DIARY
or
INTELLIGENCE SUMMARY
(Erase heading not required.)

Sheet II   Vol XXXIII   Ref 26/F 14 d 10.38

Place	1919 Date	Hour	Summary of Events and Information	Remarks and references to Appendices
Marquise	Mar Rd		2 ORs RAMC to UK for disposal contingence men RAM	
	"17		2 ORs RAMC to UK for disposal. 1 Former Bros (RAMC) transferred to COO Bnr Frans MRS	
	"18		3 wards to Celtrity Corp for disposal. 2 ORs RAMC transferred to 157 Field Ambulance. Capt W.H. Mann	
			MR C (USA) left for disposal. Major J. Crawford MC RAMC 135th Fd Ambulance left for duty w/ 2nd Army AKC (USA) MRS Burial	
	19		7 ORs RAMC returnable transferred to 17 CCS Bonnières. Capt C.W. McClanahan ARC (USA) reports for duty. Lieut S.F. Brackley RAMC 107 Fd ambulance attd left for duty w/ 2nd Army (prov)	
	20		1 OR RASC (MT) transferred to COO Bn MT Col. for disposal (arr)	
	21		2 ORs returnable RAMC transferred to 11 CCS. 1 Bro RAMC transferred to COO Bn Frans	
	24		5 MR Ambs to Celtrity Corp for disposal.	
	26		Capt H.O. Knopf deathless while on leave to UK. 1 OR NCO transferred to DGMS cour	
	27		Capt C.W. McClanahan left for disposal. Casualty Return (called returns for duty) KMS	
	29		a/Lt Col T.R. Huddleston RAMC Capt H.Rimer Dwhd Transport to Lille Centre transfer men Jf transfd (prov)	
	30		Capt H.Rimer RAMC attached for temp duty w/ Lance men RAM	
	31		Hostel attn cancel. Lt Col H. Ruan Pollock, Historian officer ramc ramc "proceeded to England for disposal" o.c. 136 Field Ambulance Cadre	

136 v. 7. 4.

17 JUL 1919

WAR DIARY or INTELLIGENCE SUMMARY

Army Form C. 2118

Vol: XXXIV 136 Fd Amb
Map. Ref:- Sheet 36/L3 d 50.30

Place	Date	Hour	Summary of Events and Information	Remarks and references to Appendices
Croix	1-4-19		Assumed temporary command of Cadre. MFRP	
	7-4-19		Cadre moved from Monveaux (Sheet 36/F.14 d 10.30) to Croix (36/L3 d 50.30) MFRP. Handed over Command to Capt B. Allison R.A.M.C. & proceeded to U.K. to disposal. H. Rivers Pollock Capt RAMC O.C. 136 Field Ambce Cadre	
Gurr	8/4/19		Assumed command of Cadre RA	
	14/4/19		1 O.R. (RAMC) to U.K. for disposal RA	
	25/4/19		1/Capt & Mr W. Godley M.C. left for disposal in U.K. B Allinson Capt RAMC O.C. 136 F.A. Cadre	

No 136

Army Form C. 2118

136 Fd Amb

WAR DIARY
or
INTELLIGENCE SUMMARY

Vol XXV Map Ref: Sheet 36/L3 & 50. 30

(Erase heading not required.)

Instructions regarding War Diaries and Intelligence Summaries are contained in F.S. Regs., Part II. and the Staff Manual respectively. Title Pages will be prepared in manuscript.

Place	Date	Hour	Summary of Events and Information	Remarks and references to Appendices
Croix (Nord)	6/9/19		Reductor Idade to Officer 1440 ORs continued	Censored
	13/9/19		1 N.C.O. & 2 ORs (RASC MT att) transferred to 40 F Sup train (off strgth)
	15/9/19		Instruction received to reduce RASC (M.T.) details to 70 ORs for
	20/9/19		1 Warrant Officer (RASC M.T. att) transferred & 287 by RASC off strgth for
	24/9/19		5 ORs (RASC MT att) transferred to 4 M & Ammo Train (off strgth) for
			1 VR (RASC M.T.) despatched to U.K. for dispersal for
	29/9/19		2 Pte Batmen (2 RFA VT Ps & Shrouds att) despatched for dispersal in U.K. off strgth. for

R Wilson Capt R.A.M.C.
O/C 136 Field Ambulance

1875 Wt. W593/826 1,000,000 4/15 J.B.C. & A. A.D.S.S./Forms/C. 2118.

www.ingramcontent.com/pod-product-compliance
Lightning Source LLC
Chambersburg PA
CBHW081533160426
43191CB00011B/1751